CLASSIC
FISH
COOKING

CLASSIC
FISH
COOKING

DELICIOUS DISHES FOR
ALL OCCASIONS

Linda Doeser

HERMES
HOUSE

This paperback edition published by Hermes House
an imprint of

Anness Publishing Limited
Hermes House, 88–89 Blackfriars Road
London SE1 8HA

Publisher: Joanna Lorenz
Copy Editor: Leslie Viney
Designer: Mason Linklater
Illustrations: Madeleine David

Front cover: Lisa Tai, Designer; Thomas Odulate, Photographer;
Helen Trent, Stylist; Joy Skipper, Home Economist

Recipes: Catherine Atkinson, Alex Barker, Ruby Le Bois, Carla Capalbo,
Maxine Clark, Christine France, Carole Handslip, Sarah Gates, Shirley Gill,
Norma MacMillan, Sue Maggs, Katherine Richmond, Jenny Stacey, Liz Trigg, Hilaire Walden, Lara Washburn, Steven
Wheeler
Photographers: Karl Adamson, Edward Allwright, Steve Baxter, James Duncan, John Freeman, Michelle Garrett, Amanda
Heywood, Don Last

Previously published as part of a larger compendium, *The Great Fish & Shellfish Cookbook*

Printed and bound in Hong Kong/China

1 3 5 7 9 10 8 6 4 2

NOTES
Standard spoon and cup measurements are level.

Medium eggs should be used unless otherwise stated.

CONTENTS

Introduction

The variety of fish and seafood is almost endless and, as fish combines superbly with just about every other imaginable ingredient, the choice of classic dishes is almost bewildering. This mouth-watering collection has been inspired by great fish dishes from all over the world – French Bouillabaisse, Italian Roast Sea Bass, Russian Salmon Coulibiac, Turkish Cold Fish, Indian Fish Stew, Louisiana Seafood Gumbo, Chinese Seafood Chow Mein and Spanish Seafood Paella, to name only some.

While some recipes are elaborate or even expensive, many of the best classic fish dishes are astonishingly simple and economical, taking full advantage of the natural flavours and textures of the ingredients. An additional benefit is the high nutritional value of fish. It is packed with protein, vitamins and minerals and is thought to help lower blood cholesterol levels. What is more, fish and seafood are best cooked quickly, so even pies and casseroles take relatively little time.

The information-packed introduction provides step-by-step instructions for skinning and filleting fish and preparing seafood, as well as making fish stock. The recipes are divided into five chapters – Soups & Starters, Pies & Bakes, Fried & Grilled Dishes, Casseroles & Stews and Pasta, Noodle & Rice Dishes. Each one incorporates a wide variety of fish from haddock to salmon and from scallops to squid. Hints and tips throughout the book provide additional advice on alternative ingredients and techniques.

Boning Round Fish for Stuffing

1 Gut the fish through the stomach as described on the previous page.

2 Slit the fish on either side of the backbone, cutting the flesh away from the bone until it is completely detached.

3 With a heavy pair of scissors, snip the backbone once at the head and once at the tail.

4 Lift out the bone.

Boning a Round Fish Through the Stomach

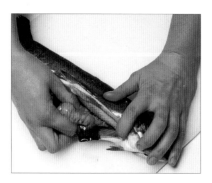

1 Gut the fish through the stomach as previously described. Continue the stomach slit on one side of the backbone as far as the tail.

2 Open the cavity and remove the insides.

3 Clean the insides of the fish, wiping away any remaining blood or guts.

4 Open the cavity and, with the blade of the knife, cut away the loose inside bones that line the flesh.

5 Turn the fish over and slit the flesh at the base of the backbone on the other side.

6 With the blade of the knife, cut loose the inside bones lining the flesh in the same way as the first side.

7 Carefully loosen the backbone of the fish completely.

8 With scissors, snip the backbone at the head and the tail.

9 Carefully peel the backbone away from the flesh with any inside bones.

10 The head can be kept and the two side fillets rolled in spirals, skin side inwards. Alternatively, fold the skin outwards and tuck the tail inside.

11 Alternatively, the head and skin can be removed and the fillets rolled or cooked flat.

Cutting Steaks and Cutlets

1 With a large, sharp knife, slice the fish across, at a right angle to the backbone, into slices of the desired thickness.

2 If necessary, cut through the backbone with kitchen scissors or a knife with a serrated blade.

COOK'S TIP

Round fish and large flat fish, such as halibut, are often cut into steaks and cutlets for cooking. Steaks are cut from the tail end of the fish, while cutlets are cut from the centre. They are usually cut about 2.5–4cm/1–1½in thick.

Filleting Round Fish

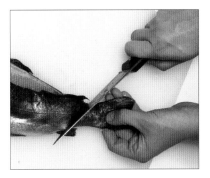

1 Holding the knife horizontally, slit the skin from head to tail along one side of the backbone.

3 Holding the knife flat and keeping the blade in contact with the bone, cut away the flesh from head to tail in a continuous slicing motion.

5 Trim off the tail.

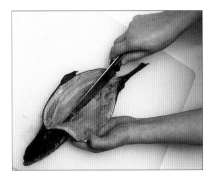

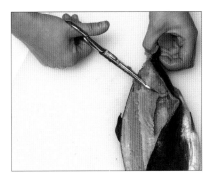

2 Cut down to the backbone just behind the fish's head.

4 Cut the backbone at the tail end with scissors.

6 Cut the fish into two fillets.

Skinning a Fillet

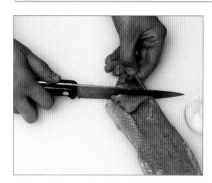

1 Secure the fillet with salt on a chopping board. Insert a sharp, flexible knife at the end of the fillet and hold securely.

2 Working in a cutting motion against the skin, move the knife along the fillet.

3 Continue until the skin has been completely removed from the flesh.

Boning Flat Fish

1 Using a flexible knife, cut along the backbone.

2 Cut the flesh away from the bones, holding the knife almost parallel to them.

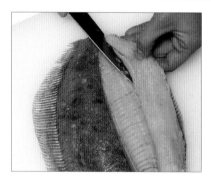

3 Cut to the edge of the transverse bones, but do not remove the fillet completely.

4 Turn the fish over and repeat for the opposite fillet.

5 Fold both fillets out.

6 Using a strong pair of scissors, cut the bones along the edges.

7 Loosen the bones away from the flesh.

8 With kitchen scissors, snip the backbone at both the head and the tail ends.

9 Lift the backbone at the tail end and pull, stripping it from the flesh underneath.

Filleting Flat Fish

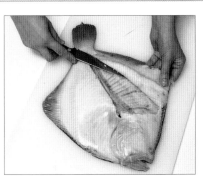

3 Turn the fish over and cut a straight line from the tail to the head as before.

4 Work the flesh away from the bones as described in steps 1 and 2, and then repeat with the fourth fillet.

1 With a sharp knife, cut around the edge of the fish to outline the shape of the fillets. Cut a straight line from the tail to the head along the spine through the bone. Keeping the knife almost flat, slip it between the flesh and the rib bones.

2 Cut away the fillet, using a stroking motion and keeping the knife flat. Continue cutting until the fillet and flesh against the fins has been detached with the skin in one piece. Continue with the other fillet.

Skinning Flat Fish

1 Lay the fish on a chopping board, dark side uppermost. With a sharp knife held at an angle, cut across the skin where the tail joins the body, taking care not to cut all the way through.

2 With the knife still held at an angle, start to cut. Keep the fish secure on the board with some salt and gradually prise the flap of skin away from the flesh. When you have a good flap of skin, grasp it with one hand and hold the other end of the fish with your other hand. Firmly pull the skin towards the head.

Fish Stock

675g/1½lb head, bones and trimmings
    from white fish
1 onion, sliced
2 celery sticks with leaves, chopped
1 carrot, sliced
½ lemon, sliced (optional)
1 bay leaf
3–4 fresh parsley sprigs
6 black peppercorns
1.3 litres/2¼ pints/5½ cups water
120ml/4fl oz/½ cup dry white wine

1 Rinse the fish heads, bones and trimmings under cold running water. Put them in a large saucepan with the vegetables, lemon, if using, herbs, peppercorns, water and wine. Bring to the boil, skimming the surface frequently. Reduce the heat and simmer for 25 minutes.

2 Strain the stock, but do not press down on the contents of the strainer. If you are not using the stock immediately, leave to cool and then refrigerate. Fish stock should be used within 2 days. It may be frozen and kept for up to 3 months.

Preparing Mussels and Clams

Molluscs, such as mussels and clams, should be eaten very fresh and should be alive when you buy and cook them (unless they have been shelled and frozen or are canned). You can tell if they are alive because their shells are tightly closed. Any that are open, should shut at once when tapped sharply with a knife. Any that do not close or that have broken shells should be discarded.

If you have collected the shellfish yourself, leave them to stand in a bucket of sea water for several hours, changing the water once or twice. Do not use fresh water, as it will kill them. Add one or two handfuls of cornmeal or flour to the water to help clean the stomachs of the shellfish. Shellfish bought from a shop will already have been purged of sand.

1 Scrub the shells with a stiff brush and rinse well. This can be done under cold running water.

2 Pull off the 'beards' (their anchor threads) with the help of a small knife. Rinse well.

3 To steam, put a little dry white wine or water in a large saucepan, together with any flavourings specified in the recipe. Add the mussels or clams, cover tightly and bring to the boil. Cook for 5–10 minutes, or until the shells open, shaking the pan from time to time. Discard any that do not open.

4 Serve the shellfish in the shells or shell them before using. Strain the cooking liquid, which includes the liquor from the shells, and spoon it over the shellfish or use it as the basis for a sauce.

5 To open a live clam or mussel, hold it in one hand with the hinge in your palm. Insert the side of a clam or oyster knife blade between the shell halves and work it round to cut through the hinge muscle.

6 Open the shell and cut the clam or mussel free of the shell. Do this over a bowl to catch all the liquor from the shell.

Opening and Cleaning Scallops

1 To open the shell, hold the scallop with the flat shell uppermost. Probe between the shells with a short knife to find a small opening. Insert the blade and run it across the roof of the shell.

2 Separate the two halves of the shell, and pull apart.

3 Slide the blade under the greyish outer rim of the flesh, called the skirt, to free the scallop. Pull away the muscle with a small knife. Use the trimmed scallop, whole or halved, for cooking.

Opening Oysters

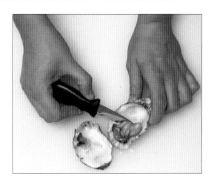

1 Place the oyster, wrapped in a clean napkin or tea towel, on a firm surface with the flatter shell uppermost and the hinge towards you. Holding the oyster with one hand, insert the tip of an oyster knife into the gap in the hinge.

2 Twist the blade to snap the shells apart.

3 Continue to hold the oyster firmly in the cloth and slide the blade along the inside of the upper shell to sever the muscle that holds the shell together. Discard the top shell and lift the lower rounded shell off the napkin, making sure the liquid in it does not spill. Clean any bits of broken shell with the point of the knife.

4 Grip the lower shell firmly with your fingers. Cutting towards yourself, run the blade under the oyster to sever the muscle attaching it to the lower shell and free it.

Preparing and Deveining Prawns

Prawns may be cooked in their shells, but are often peeled first. The shells can be used to make an aromatic stock. The intestinal vein that runs down the back is usually removed from large prawns, mainly because of its appearance, but also because it may contain grit which makes it unpleasant to eat. Prawns may be sold with the heads on. These are easily pulled off with the fingers and will enhance the flavour of stock made with their shells.

1 Holding the prawn firmly in one hand, pull off the legs with the fingers of the other hand.

2 Peel the shell away from the body. When you reach the tail, hold the body and pull away the tail; the shell will come off with it. Alternatively, you can leave the tail on the prawn and just remove the body shell.

3 Make a shallow cut down the centre of the curved back of the prawn. Pull out the black vein with a cocktail stick or your fingers.

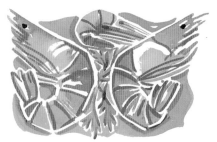

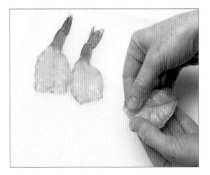

4 To make butterfly prawns, cut along the deveining slit to split open the prawn, without cutting all the way through. Open up the prawn flat.

5 To devein prawns in their shells, insert a cocktail stick crossways in several places along the back where the shell overlaps to lift out the vein.

SOUPS &
STARTERS

Classic Italian Fish Soup

Liguria is famous for its fish soups. In this one the fish are cooked in a broth with vegetables and then puréed. This soup can also be used to dress pasta.

INGREDIENTS

Serves 6

1kg/2¼lb mixed fish or fish pieces, such as
    coley, dogfish, whiting, red mullet,
    pollock or cod
90ml/6 tbsp olive oil, plus extra to serve
1 medium onion, finely chopped
1 stick celery, chopped
1 carrot, chopped
60ml/4 tbsp chopped fresh parsley
175ml/6fl oz/¾ cup dry white wine
3 medium tomatoes, skinned and chopped
2 garlic cloves, finely chopped
1.5 litres/2½ pints/6¼ cups boiling water
salt and freshly ground black pepper
rounds of French bread, to serve

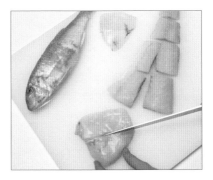

1 Scale and clean the fish, discarding all the innards, but leaving the heads on. Cut into large pieces. Rinse well in cool water.

2 Heat the oil in a large saucepan and add the onion. Cook over low to moderate heat until it begins to soften. Stir in the celery and carrot, and cook for 5 minutes more. Add the parsley.

3 Pour in the wine, raise the heat, and cook until it reduces by about half. Stir in the tomatoes and garlic. Cook for 3–4 minutes, stirring occasionally. Pour in the boiling water, and bring back to the boil. Cook over moderate heat for 15 minutes.

4 Stir in the fish, and simmer for 10–15 minutes, or until the fish are tender. Season with salt and pepper.

5 Remove the fish from the soup with a slotted spoon. Discard the heads and any bones. Purée in a food processor. Taste for seasoning. If the soup is too thick, add a little more water.

6 To serve, heat the soup to simmering. Toast the rounds of French bread, and sprinkle with olive oil. Place 2 or 3 in the base of each soup plate before pouring over the soup.

Smoked Haddock and Potato Soup

The traditional name for this soup is 'cullen skink'. A cullen is the 'seatown' or port district of a town, while 'skink' means stock or broth.

Serves 6

1 finnan haddock, about 350g/12oz

1 onion, chopped

bouquet garni

900ml/1½ pints/3¾ cups water

500g/1¼ lb potatoes, quartered

600ml/1 pint/2½ cups milk

40g/1½oz butter

salt and freshly ground black pepper

snipped chives, to garnish

1 Put the haddock, onion, bouquet garni and water into a large saucepan and bring to the boil. Skim the scum from the surface, then cover the pan. Reduce the heat and poach for 10–15 minutes, until the haddock flakes easily.

COOK'S TIP

Finnan haddock is a small, whole fish that has been soaked in brine and then cold smoked.

---

2 Lift the haddock from the pan, using a fish slice, and remove the skin and bones. Flake the flesh and reserve. Return the skin and bones to the pan and simmer, uncovered, for 30 minutes.

3 Strain the fish stock and return to the pan, then add the potatoes and simmer for about 25 minutes, or until tender. Remove the potatoes from the pan using a slotted spoon. Add the milk to the pan and bring to the boil.

4 Meanwhile, mash the potatoes with the butter, then whisk into the milk in the pan until thick and creamy. Add the flaked fish to the pan and adjust the seasoning. Sprinkle with chives and serve at once with crusty bread.

Corn and Scallop Chowder

Fresh ears of corn are ideal for this chowder, although canned or frozen corn also works well. This soup makes a perfect lunch dish.

INGREDIENTS

Serves 4–6

2 ears of corn or 200g/7oz frozen or
   canned corn

600ml/1pint/2½ cups milk

15g/½oz butter or margarine

1 small leek or onion, chopped

1 small garlic clove, crushed

40g/1½oz smoked lean bacon,
   finely chopped

1 small green pepper, seeded and diced

1 celery stick, chopped

1 medium potato, diced

15ml/1 tbsp plain flour

300ml/½ pint/1¼ cups chicken or
   vegetable stock

4 scallops

115g/4oz cooked fresh mussels

pinch of paprika

150ml/¼ pint/⅔ cup single
   cream (optional)

salt and freshly ground black pepper

1 Using a sharp knife, slice down the ears of the corn to remove the kernels. Place half of the kernels in a food processor or blender and process with a little of the milk.

2 Melt the butter or margarine in a large saucepan and gently fry the leek or onion, garlic and bacon for 4–5 minutes until the leek is soft but not browned. Add the green pepper, chopped celery and diced potato and sweat over low heat for a further 3–4 minutes, stirring frequently.

3 Stir in the flour and cook for 1–2 minutes until the mixture is golden and frothy. Gradually stir in the milk and corn mixture, stock, the remaining milk and corn kernels and seasoning.

4 Bring to the boil, then reduce the heat and simmer, partially covered, for 15–20 minutes until the vegetables are tender.

5 Pull the corals away from the scallops and slice the white flesh into 5mm/¼ in slices. Stir the scallops into the soup, cook for 4 minutes and then stir in the corals, mussels and paprika. Heat through for a few minutes and then stir in the cream, if using. Adjust the seasoning to taste and serve.

Bouillabaisse

Perhaps the most famous of all Mediterranean fish soups, this recipe, originating from Marseilles in the south of France, is a rich and colourful mixture of fish and shellfish, flavoured with tomatoes, saffron and orange.

INGREDIENTS

Serves 4–6

1.5kg/3-3½lb mixed fish and raw shellfish, such as red mullet, John Dory, monkfish, red snapper, whiting, large raw prawns and clams

225g/8oz well-flavoured tomatoes

pinch of saffron strands

90ml/6 tbsp olive oil

1 onion, sliced

1 leek, sliced

1 celery stick, sliced

2 garlic cloves, crushed

1 bouquet garni

1 strip orange rind

2.5ml/½ tsp fennel seeds

15ml/1 tbsp tomato purée

10ml/2 tsp Pernod

salt and freshly ground black pepper

4–6 thick slices French bread and 45ml/ 3 tbsp chopped fresh parsley, to serve

1 Remove the heads, tails and fins from the fish and set the fish aside. Put the trimmings in a large pan, with 1.2 litres/2 pints/ 5 cups water. Bring to the boil, and simmer for 15 minutes. Strain, and reserve the liquid.

2 Cut the fish into large chunks. Leave the shellfish in their shells. Scald the tomatoes, then drain and refresh in cold water. Peel and roughly chop them. Soak the saffron in 15–30ml/1–2 tbsp hot water.

3 Heat the oil in a large pan, add the onion, leek and celery and cook until softened. Add the garlic, bouquet garni, orange rind, fennel seeds and tomatoes, then stir in the saffron and soaking liquid and the fish stock. Season with salt and pepper, then bring to the boil and simmer for 30–40 minutes.

4 Add the shellfish and boil for about 6 minutes. Add the fish and cook for a further 6–8 minutes, until it flakes easily.

5 Using a slotted spoon, transfer the fish to a warmed serving platter. Keep the liquid boiling, to allow the oil to emulsify with the broth. Add the tomato purée and Pernod, then check the seasoning. To serve, place a slice of French bread in the base of each soup bowl, pour the broth over the top and serve the fish separately, sprinkled with the parsley.

COOK'S TIP

Saffron comes from the orange and red stigmas of a type of crocus. These must be harvested by hand and it requires about 250,000 crocus flowers for a yield of 500g/1¼lb saffron. Consequently, it is extremely expensive – the highest-priced spice in the world. However, its slightly bitter flavour and pleasantly sweet aroma are unique and cannot be replaced by any other spice. It is an essential ingredient in all traditional versions of bouillabaisse and should not be omitted.

Prawn Bisque

The classic French method for making a bisque requires pushing the shellfish through a tamis, or drum sieve. This is much simpler and the result is just as smooth.

INGREDIENTS

Serves 6–8

675g/1½lb small or medium cooked
    prawns in the shell
25ml/1½ tbsp vegetable oil
2 onions, halved and sliced
1 large carrot, sliced
2 celery sticks, sliced
2 litres/3⅓ pints/8 cups water
a few drops of lemon juice
30ml/2 tbsp tomato purée
bouquet garni
50g/2oz butter
50g/2oz plain flour
45–60ml/3–4 tbsp brandy
150ml/¼ pint/⅔ cup whipping cream
salt and freshly ground white pepper
flat leaf parsley sprig, to garnish

1 Remove the heads and peel away the shells from the prawns, reserving them for the stock. Chill the prawns.

2 Heat the oil in a large saucepan, add the prawn heads and shells and cook over a high heat, stirring frequently, until they start to brown. Reduce the heat to medium, add the onions, carrot and celery and fry gently, stirring occasionally, for about 5 minutes until the onions start to soften.

3 Add the water, lemon juice, tomato purée and bouquet garni. Bring the stock to the boil, then reduce the heat, cover and simmer gently for 25 minutes. Strain the stock through a sieve.

4 Melt the butter in a heavy saucepan over a medium heat. Stir in the flour and cook until just golden, stirring occasionally. Add the brandy and gradually pour in about half of the prawn stock, whisking vigorously until smooth, then whisk in the remaining liquid. Season to taste. Reduce the heat, cover and simmer for 5 minutes, stirring frequently.

5 Strain the soup into a clean saucepan. Add the cream and a little extra lemon juice to taste, if wished, then stir in most of the reserved prawns and cook over a medium heat until hot. Serve at once, garnished with the reserved prawns and parsley.

Hot-and-sour Prawn Soup

How hot this soup is depends on the type of chilli used. Try tiny Thai chillies if you really want to go for the burn.

INGREDIENTS

Serves 6

225g/8oz raw prawns

2 lemon grass stalks

1.5 litres/2½ pints/6¼ cups vegetable stock

4 kaffir lime leaves

2 slices peeled fresh root ginger

60ml/4 tbsp Thai fish sauce

60ml/4 tbsp fresh lime juice

2 garlic cloves, crushed

6 spring onions, chopped

1 fresh red chilli, seeded and cut
    into strips

115g/4oz/generous 1½ cups oyster
    mushrooms, sliced

fresh coriander leaves and kaffir lime
    slices, to garnish

1 Peel and devein the prawns and set them aside. Put the shells in a large saucepan.

COOK'S TIP

Large tiger prawns are best for this recipe. They are sometimes available fresh, which have the best flavour, or frozen. It is important that they are not overcooked, or they will become unpleasantly tough.

2 Lightly crush the lemon grass and add the stalks to the pan, together with the vegetable stock, kaffir lime leaves and slices of ginger. Bring to the boil, lower the heat and simmer for 20 minutes.

3 Strain the stock into a clean pan, discarding the prawn shells and flavourings. Add the fish sauce, lime juice, garlic, spring onions, chilli and mushrooms. Bring to the boil, lower the heat and simmer for 5 minutes. Add the prawns and cook for 2–3 minutes. Garnish with coriander and lime slices and serve.

Seafood Pancakes

The combination of fresh and smoked haddock imparts a wonderful flavour to the filling.

INGREDIENTS

Serves 4–6

For the pancakes

115g/4oz plain flour

pinch of salt

1 egg, plus 1 egg yolk

300ml/½ pint/1¼ cups milk

15ml/1 tbsp melted butter, plus extra for
    cooking

50–75g/2–3oz Gruyère cheese, grated

curly salad leaves, to serve

For the filling

225g/8oz smoked haddock fillet

225g/8oz fresh haddock fillet

300ml/½ pint/1¼ cups milk

150ml/¼ pint/⅔ cup single cream

40g/1½oz butter

40g/1½oz plain flour

freshly grated nutmeg

2 hard-boiled eggs, shelled and chopped

salt and freshly ground black pepper

1 To make the pancakes, sift the flour and salt into a bowl. Make a well in the centre and add the egg and egg yolk. Whisk the eggs, starting to incorporate some of the flour from around the edges.

2 Gradually add the milk, whisking all the time, until the batter is smooth and has the consistency of thin cream. Stir in the melted butter.

3 Heat a small crêpe pan or omelette pan until hot, then rub round the inside of the pan with a pad of kitchen paper dipped in melted butter.

4 Pour about 30ml/2 tbsp of the batter into the pan, then tip the pan to coat the base evenly. Cook for about 30 seconds until the underside of the pancake is golden brown.

5 Flip the pancake over and cook the other side until lightly browned. Repeat to make 12 pancakes, rubbing the pan with melted butter between cooking each pancake. Stack the pancakes as you make them between sheets of greaseproof paper. Keep warm on a plate set over a pan of simmering water.

6 Put the smoked and fresh haddock fillets in a large pan. Add the milk and poach for 6–8 minutes, until just tender. Lift out the fish using a slotted spoon and, when cool enough to handle, remove the skin and any bones. Reserve the milk.

7 Pour the single cream into a measuring jug, then strain enough of the reserved milk into the jug to make the quantity up to 450ml/¾ pint/1⅞ cups.

8 Melt the butter in a pan, stir in the flour and cook gently for 1 minute. Gradually mix in the milk mixture, stirring continuously, to make a smooth sauce. Cook for 2–3 minutes, until thickened. Season with salt, pepper and nutmeg. Roughly flake the haddock and fold into the sauce with the eggs. Leave to cool.

9 Divide the filling among the pancakes. Fold the sides of each pancake into the centre, then roll them up so that the filling is completely enclosed.

10 Butter four or six individual ovenproof dishes and arrange 2–3 filled pancakes in each, or butter one large dish for all the pancakes. Brush with melted butter and cook in a preheated oven at 180°C/350°F/ Gas 4 for 15 minutes. Sprinkle over the Gruyère and cook for a further 5 minutes, until warmed through. Serve hot with a few curly salad leaves.

VARIATION

To ring the changes, add cooked, peeled prawns, smoked mussels or cooked fresh, shelled mussels to the filling, instead of the chopped hard-boiled eggs.

Scallops Wrapped in Parma Ham

This is a delicious summer recipe for cooking over the barbecue.

INGREDIENTS

Serves 4

24 medium-size scallops, without corals,
    prepared for cooking
lemon juice
8–12 slices Parma ham
olive oil
freshly ground black pepper
lemon wedges, to serve

1 Preheat the grill or prepare a charcoal fire. Sprinkle the scallops with lemon juice. Cut the Parma ham into long strips. Wrap one strip around each scallop. Thread them on to 8 skewers.

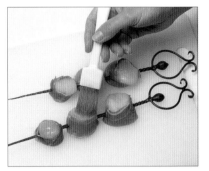

2 Brush with oil. Arrange on a baking sheet if grilling. Cook about 10cm/4in from the heat under a preheated grill for 3–5 minutes on each side or until the scallops are opaque and tender. Alternatively, cook over charcoal, turning once, until the scallops are opaque and tender.

3 Set 2 skewers on each plate. Sprinkle the scallops with freshly ground black pepper and serve with lemon wedges.

COOK'S TIP

The edible parts of the scallop are the round white muscle and the coral or roe. When preparing fresh scallops, keep the skirt – the frilly part – for making stock.

Coquilles St Jacques au Gratin

This dish has been a classic on bistro menus since Hemingway's days in Paris – it makes an appealing starter, but could also be served as a rich and elegant main course.

INGREDIENTS

Serves 2–4

250ml/8fl oz/1 cup dry white wine
125ml/4fl oz/½ cup water
2 shallots, finely chopped
1 bay leaf
450g/1lb shelled scallops, rinsed
40g/1½oz/3 tbsp butter
40g/1½oz/⅓ cup plain flour
90ml/6 tbsp whipping cream
freshly grated nutmeg
175g/6oz mushrooms, thinly sliced
45–60ml/3–4 tbsp dry breadcrumbs
salt and freshly ground black pepper

1 Combine the wine, water, shallots and bay leaf in a medium saucepan. Bring to the boil, reduce the heat and simmer for 10 minutes. Add the scallops, cover and simmer for 3–4 minutes, until they are opaque.

2 Remove the scallops from the cooking liquid with a slotted spoon. Boil the liquid until reduced to 175ml/6fl oz/¾ cup. Strain into a bowl and set aside.

3 Carefully pull off the tough muscle from the side of the scallops and discard. Slice the scallops in half crossways.

4 Melt 30g/1oz/2 tbsp of the butter in a heavy saucepan over a medium heat. Stir in the flour and cook for 2 minutes. Add the reserved cooking liquid, whisking vigorously until smooth, then whisk in the cream and season to taste with salt, pepper and nutmeg. Reduce the heat and simmer, stirring frequently, for 10 minutes.

5 Melt the remaining butter in a frying pan over a medium heat. Add the sliced mushrooms and cook, stirring frequently, for about 5 minutes, until they are lightly browned. Stir the mushrooms into the sauce.

6 Preheat the grill. Add the scallops to the sauce and adjust the seasoning. Spoon the mixture into four individual gratin dishes, large scallop shells or a flameproof dish and sprinkle evenly with breadcrumbs. Grill until golden brown and bubbly and serve.

Smoked Salmon Terrine with Lemons

Lemons can be cut and sliced in so many ways. This melt-in-the-mouth smoked salmon terrine gives a time-honoured accompaniment an intriguing new twist.

INGREDIENTS

Serves 6
4 sheets of leaf gelatine
60ml/4 tbsp water
400g/14oz smoked salmon, sliced
300g/11oz/1½ cups cream cheese
120ml/4fl oz/½ cup crème fraîche
30ml/2 tbsp dill mustard
juice of 1 lime

For the garnish
2 lemons
piece of muslin
raffia, for tying

1 Soak the gelatine in the water in a small bowl until softened. Meanwhile, line a 450g/1lb loaf tin with clear film. Use some of the smoked salmon to line the tin, laying the slices widthways across the base and up the sides and leaving enough overlap to fold over the top of the filling.

2 Set aside enough of the remaining smoked salmon to make a middle layer the length of the tin. Chop the rest finely by hand or in a food processor. Beat together the cream cheese, crème fraîche and dill mustard with the chopped smoked salmon until everything is well combined.

3 Squeeze out the gelatine and melt gently in a small saucepan with the lime juice. Add to the smoked salmon mixture and mix thoroughly. Spoon half the mixture into the lined tin. Lay the reserved smoked salmon slices on the mixture along the length of the tin, then spoon on the rest of the filling and smooth the top.

4 Tap the tin on the work surface to expel any trapped air. Fold over the overhanging salmon slices to cover the top. Cover with clear film and chill for at least 4 hours.

5 Make the garnish. Cut 1 lemon in half widthways. Wrap each half in a small square of muslin. Gather the muslin at the rounded end of the lemon and tie neatly with raffia.

6 Cut a small 'V' from the side of the other lemon. Repeat at 5mm/¼in intervals. Turn out the terrine, then slice. Garnish with muslin-wrapped lemons and lemon 'leaves'.

Deep-fried Whitebait

A spicy coating on these fish gives this favourite dish a crunchy bite.

INGREDIENTS

Serves 6

115g/4oz plain flour

2.5ml/½ tsp curry powder

2.5ml/½ tsp ground ginger

2.5ml/½ tsp ground cayenne pepper

pinch of salt

1.1kg/2½lb fresh or frozen
  whitebait, thawed

vegetable oil for deep-frying

lemon wedges, to garnish

1 Mix together the flour, spices and salt in a large bowl.

2 Coat the fish in the seasoned flour and shake off any excess.

3 Heat the oil in a large, heavy-based saucepan until it reaches a temperature of 190°C/375°F. Fry the whitebait in batches for about 2–3 minutes until the fish is golden and crispy.

4 Drain well on absorbent kitchen paper. Serve hot, garnished with lemon wedges.

Crab and Ricotta Tartlets

Use the meat from a freshly cooked crab, weighing about 450g/1lb, if you can. Otherwise, look out for frozen brown and white crab meat.

INGREDIENTS

Serves 4

225g/8oz plain flour

115g/4oz butter, diced

about 60ml/4 tbsp iced water

225g/8oz ricotta

15ml/1 tbsp grated onion

30ml/2 tbsp grated Parmesan cheese

2.5ml/½ tsp mustard powder

2 eggs, plus 1 egg yolk

225g/8oz crab meat

30ml/2 tbsp chopped fresh parsley

2.5–5ml/½–1 tsp anchovy essence

5–10ml/1–2 tsp lemon juice

salt and cayenne pepper

salad leaves, to garnish

1 Sift the flour and a good pinch of salt into a mixing bowl, add the diced butter and rub it in with your fingertips, until the mixture resembles fine breadcrumbs. Gradually stir in enough iced water to make a firm dough.

2 Turn the dough on to a floured surface and knead lightly. Roll out the pastry and use to line four 10cm/4in tartlet tins. Prick the bases with a fork, then chill in the refrigerator for 30 minutes.

3 Line the pastry cases with greaseproof paper and fill with baking beans. Bake in a preheated oven at 200°C/400°F/Gas 6 for 10 minutes, then remove the paper and beans. Return to the oven and bake for a further 10 minutes.

4 Place the ricotta, grated onion, Parmesan and mustard in a bowl and beat until soft. Gradually beat in the eggs and egg yolk.

5 Gently stir in the crab meat and chopped parsley, then add the anchovy essence, lemon juice, salt and cayenne pepper, to taste.

6 Remove the tartlet cases from the oven and reduce the temperature to 180°C/350°F/Gas 4. Spoon the filling into the cases and bake for 20 minutes, until set and golden brown. Serve hot with a garnish of salad leaves.

Prawn and Artichoke Salad

Artichokes are very popular in Louisiana, where this recipe comes from – and the local cooks are quite willing to use canned hearts.

INGREDIENTS

Serves 4

1 garlic clove
10ml/2 tsp Dijon mustard
60ml/4 tbsp red wine vinegar
150ml/¼ pint/⅔ cup olive oil
45ml/3 tbsp shredded fresh basil leaves or
    30ml/2 tbsp finely chopped
    fresh parsley
1 red onion, very finely sliced
350g/12oz cooked peeled prawns
400g/14oz can artichoke hearts
½ head iceberg lettuce
salt and freshly ground black pepper

1 Coarsely chop the garlic, then crush it to a pulp with 5ml/ 1 tsp salt, using the flat of a heavy knife blade.

2 Mix the garlic and mustard to a paste, then beat in the vinegar and finally the olive oil, beating hard to make a thick creamy dressing. Season with freshly ground black pepper and, if necessary, additional salt.

3 Stir the fresh basil or parsley into the dressing, followed by the sliced onion. Leave to stand for 30 minutes at room temperature, then stir in the prawns and chill in the refrigerator for 1 hour or until ready to serve.

4 Drain the artichoke hearts and halve each one. Shred the lettuce finely.

5 Make a bed of lettuce on a serving platter or 4 individual salad plates and spread the artichoke hearts over it.

6 Immediately before serving, pour the prawns and onion and their marinade over the top of the salad.

Mussels Steamed in White Wine

This is the best and easiest way to serve the small tender mussels, bouchots, which are farmed along much of the French coast line. Serve with plenty of crusty French bread to dip in the juices.

INGREDIENTS

Serves 4

1.75kg/4–4½lb mussels

300ml/½ pint/1¼ cups dry white wine

4–6 large shallots, finely chopped

bouquet garni

freshly ground black pepper

1 Discard any broken mussels and those with open shells that do not close immediately when tapped sharply. Under cold running water, scrape the mussel shells with a knife to remove any barnacles and pull out the stringy 'beards'. Soak the mussels in several changes of cold water for at least 1 hour.

2 In a large, heavy, flameproof casserole combine the white wine, shallots, bouquet garni and plenty of pepper. Bring to the boil over a medium-high heat and cook for 2 minutes.

3 Add the mussels to the casserole, cover tightly and cook, shaking and tossing the pan occasionally, for 5 minutes, or until the mussels have opened. Discard any mussels that have not opened.

4 Using a slotted spoon, divide the mussels among 4 warmed soup plates. Tilt the casserole a little and hold for a few seconds to allow any sand to sink to the bottom and settle. Alternatively, strain the cooking liquid through clean muslin.

5 Spoon or pour the cooking liquid over the mussels and serve at once.

VARIATION

For Mussels with Cream Sauce, cook the shellfish as described here, but transfer the mussels to a warmed bowl and cover to keep warm. Strain the cooking liquid through a muslin-lined sieve into a large saucepan and boil for about 7–10 minutes to reduce by half. Stir in 90ml/6 tbsp whipping cream and 30ml/2 tbsp chopped fresh parsley, then add the mussels. Cook for about 1 minute more to reheat the mussels.

PIES & BAKES

~

Creamy Fish and Mushroom Pie

*Fish pie is a healthy and hearty dish
for a hungry family. To help the fish
go further, mushrooms provide both
flavour and nourishment.*

INGREDIENTS

Serves 4

225g/8oz assorted wild and cultivated
   mushrooms, such as oyster, button,
   chanterelle or St George's mushrooms,
   trimmed and quartered
675g/1½lb cod or haddock fillet, skinned
   and diced
600ml/1 pint/2½ cups milk, boiling

For the topping

900g/2lb floury potatoes, quartered
25g/1oz butter
150ml/¼ pint/⅔ cup milk
salt and freshly ground black pepper
grated nutmeg

For the sauce

50g/2oz unsalted butter
1 medium onion, chopped
½ celery stick, chopped
50g/2oz plain flour
10ml/2 tsp lemon juice
45ml/3 tbsp chopped fresh parsley

1 Butter an ovenproof dish,
scatter the mushrooms over
the base, add the fish and season
with salt and pepper to taste. Pour
on the boiling milk, cover the dish
and cook in a preheated oven at
200°C/400°F/Gas 6 for 20 minutes.

2 Using a slotted spoon, transfer
the fish and mushrooms to a
1.5 litre/2½ pint/6¼ cup baking
dish. Pour the poaching liquid into
a jug and set aside.

3 Meanwhile, cook the potatoes
in lightly salted boiling water
for 20 minutes. Drain and mash
with the butter and milk. Season
well with salt, pepper and nutmeg.

4 To make the sauce, melt the
butter in a saucepan, add the
onion and celery and fry until soft,
but not coloured. Stir in the flour,
then remove from the heat.

5 Gradually add the reserved
liquid, stirring until absorbed.
Return to the heat, stir and simmer
to thicken. Add the lemon juice
and parsley, season, then add to the
baking dish.

6 Top with the mashed potato
and return to the oven for
30–40 minutes until the topping is
golden brown.

Salmon Coulibiac

This is a complicated Russian dish that takes a lot of preparation, but is well worth it. Traditionally sturgeon is used, but, as this is difficult to obtain, salmon may be substituted. As a special treat, serve with shots of chilled vodka for an authentic Russian flavour.

INGREDIENTS

Serves 8

butter, for greasing
flour, for dusting
450g/1lb puff pastry
1 egg, beaten
salt and freshly ground black pepper
lemon wedges and fresh dill sprigs,
    to garnish

For the pancakes

2 eggs, separated
750ml/1¼ pints/3 cups milk
225g/8oz plain flour
350g/12oz butter, melted
2.5ml/½ tsp salt
2.5ml/½ tsp caster sugar

For the filling

50g/2oz butter
350g/12oz chestnut mushrooms, sliced
100ml/3½fl oz/scant ½ cup white wine
juice of ½ lemon
675g/1½lb salmon fillet, skinned
115g/4oz long grain rice
30ml/2 tbsp chopped fresh dill
1 large onion, chopped
4 hard-boiled eggs, shelled and sliced

1 First make the pancakes. Whisk the egg yolks together and add the milk. Gradually beat in the flour, 335g/11½oz of the melted butter, salt and sugar until smooth. Leave to stand for about 30 minutes.

2 Whisk the egg whites until they just form stiff peaks, then fold into the batter. Heat a little of the remaining butter in a heavy-based frying pan and add about 45ml/3 tbsp of the batter. Turn and cook until golden. Repeat until all the mixture has been used up, brushing on a little melted butter when stacking the pancakes. When they are cool, cut into long rectangles, cover and set aside.

3 For the filling, melt most of the butter in a heavy-based frying pan, add the mushrooms and cook for 3 minutes. Add 60ml/4 tbsp of the wine and boil for 2 minutes, then simmer for a further 5 minutes. Add almost all the remaining wine and the lemon juice.

4 Place the salmon on top of the cooked mushrooms, cover with foil, and gently steam for 8–10 minutes, until just cooked. Remove the salmon from the pan and set aside.

5 Set aside the mushrooms and pour the cooking liquid into a large clean pan. Add the rice and cook for 10–15 minutes, until tender, adding more wine if necessary. Remove from the heat and stir in the dill and seasoning. Melt the remaining butter and fry the onion until brown. Set aside.

6 Grease a large baking tray. Flour a clean dish towel, place the pastry on it and roll into a rectangle 30 x 55cm/12 x 20in. Leaving 3cm/1¼in at the top and bottom ends of the pastry, place half the pancakes in a strip up the middle of the dough. Top with half the rice, half the onion, half the eggs and half the mushrooms. Place the salmon on top of the mushrooms and press down gently. Continue the layering process in reverse.

7 Take the 3cm/1¼in ends and wrap over the filling, then fold over the long edges. Brush with beaten egg and transfer to the baking sheet, rolling it so that it ends up seam side down. Chill for 1 hour. Cut 4 small slits in the top, brush with beaten egg and bake in a preheated oven at 220°C/425°F/ Gas 7 for 10 minutes. Turn the oven down to 190°C/375°F/Gas 5 and cook for a further 30 minutes, until golden brown. Serve sliced, garnished with lemon and dill.

Stuffed Fish

Every community in India prepares stuffed fish, but the Parsi version must rank top of the list. The most popular fish in India is the pomfret. It is available from Indian grocers or large supermarkets.

INGREDIENTS

Serves 4

2 large pomfrets or Dover or lemon sole

10ml/2 tsp salt

juice of 1 lemon

slices of lime, to serve

For the masala

120ml/8 tbsp desiccated coconut

115g/4oz fresh coriander

8 fresh green chillies (or to taste)

5ml/1 tsp cumin seeds

6 garlic cloves

10ml/2 tsp caster sugar

10ml/2 tsp lemon juice

1 Scale the fish and cut off the fins. Gut the fish and remove the heads, if desired. Using a sharp knife, make 2 diagonal slashes on each side, then pat dry with kitchen paper.

2 Rub the fish inside and out with salt and lemon juice and allow to stand for 1 hour. Pat dry thoroughly with kitchen paper.

3 For the masala, grind all the ingredients together using a pestle and mortar or food processor. Stuff the fish with the masala mixture and rub any remaining masala into the gashes and all over the fish on both sides.

4 Place each fish on a separate piece of greased foil. Tightly wrap the foil over each fish. Place in a steamer and steam for 20 minutes or bake in a preheated oven at 200°C/400°F/Gas 6 for 30 minutes, or until cooked. Serve with slices of lime.

COOK'S TIP

In India, this fish dish is always steamed wrapped in banana leaves. Banana leaves are available from Indian or Chinese grocers, but vine leaves may be used instead.

Smoked Haddock Lyonnaise

Lyonnaise dishes take their name from the city of Lyons, known for its excellent food. The term 'Lyonnaise' refers to dishes prepared or garnished with onions.

INGREDIENTS

Serves 4

450g/1lb smoked haddock

150ml/¼ pint/⅔ cup milk

15g/½oz butter

2 onions, chopped

15ml/1 tbsp cornflour

150ml/¼ pint/⅔ cup Greek-style yogurt

5ml/1 tsp ground turmeric

5ml/1 tsp paprika

115g/4oz mushrooms, sliced

2 celery sticks, chopped

30ml/2 tbsp olive oil

350g/12oz firm cooked potatoes, preferably cold, diced

25–50g/1–2oz soft white breadcrumbs

salt and freshly ground black pepper

flat leaf parsley, to garnish

2 Melt the butter and fry half the chopped onions until translucent. Stir in the cornflour, then gradually blend in the fish cooking liquid and the yogurt and cook until thickened and smooth.

3 Stir in the turmeric, paprika, mushrooms and celery. Season to taste and add the flaked fish. Spoon into an ovenproof dish.

4 Heat the oil and fry the remaining onions until translucent. Add the diced potatoes and stir until lightly coated in oil. Sprinkle on the breadcrumbs and seasoning.

5 Spoon this mixture over the fish and bake in a preheated oven at 190°C/375°F/Gas 5 for 20–30 minutes.

1 Put the smoked haddock and the milk into a large pan over a low heat and poach the fish for about 15 minutes, until just cooked. Remove the haddock, reserving the cooking liquid, then flake the fish and discard the skin and any bones. Set aside.

Baked Red Snapper

The flesh of the red snapper is made tender and flavourful by rubbing in spices and baking in a sauce.

INGREDIENTS

Serves 3–4

1 large red snapper, gutted and cleaned
juice of 1 lemon
2.5ml/½ tsp paprika
2.5ml/½ tsp garlic granules
2.5ml/½ tsp dried thyme
2.5ml/½ tsp freshly ground black pepper
boiled rice and lemon wedges, to serve

For the sauce

30ml/2 tbsp palm or vegetable oil
1 onion, chopped
400g/14oz can chopped tomatoes
2 garlic cloves, crushed
1 thyme sprig or 2.5ml/½ tsp dried thyme
1 fresh green chilli, seeded and
 finely chopped
½ green pepper, seeded and chopped
300ml/½ pint/1¼ cups fish stock or water

1 Prepare the sauce. Heat the palm or vegetable oil in a saucepan, fry the onion for 5 minutes, then add the tomatoes, garlic, thyme and chilli.

2 Add the pepper and stock or water. Bring to the boil, stirring, then reduce the heat, cover and simmer for about 10 minutes, until the vegetables are soft. Leave to cool a little and then place in a blender or food processor and blend to a purée.

3 Wash the fish well and then score the skin with a sharp knife in a criss-cross pattern. Mix together the lemon juice, paprika, garlic, thyme and black pepper. Spoon the mixture over the fish and rub in well.

4 Place the fish in a greased baking dish and pour the sauce over the top. Cover with foil and bake in a preheated oven at 200°C/400°F/Gas 6 for about 30–40 minutes, or until the fish is cooked and flakes easily when tested with a knife. Serve with boiled rice and lemon wedges.

COOK'S TIP

If you prefer less sauce, remove the foil after 20 minutes and bake, uncovered, until cooked.

Fish Soufflé with Cheese Topping

This is an easy-going soufflé, which will not drop too much if kept waiting. On the other hand, it might be best to get the family seated before you take it out of the oven!

Serves 4

350g/12oz white fish, skinned and boned
150ml/¼ pint/⅔ cup milk
225g/8oz cooked potatoes, still warm
1 garlic clove, crushed
2 eggs, separated
grated rind and juice of ½ small lemon
115g/4oz cooked peeled prawns
50g/2oz grated Cheddar cheese
salt and freshly ground black pepper

1 Place the fish in a large saucepan and add the milk. Bring just to the boil, lower the heat and cook for 12 minutes, or until it flakes easily. Alternatively, place the fish and milk in a bowl and cook in the microwave for 3–4 minutes on high. Drain, reserving the milk, and place the fish in a bowl.

2 Mash the potatoes until really creamy, using as much of the reserved fish milk as necessary. Then mash in the garlic, egg yolks, lemon rind and juice and seasoning to taste.

3 Flake the fish and gently stir into the potato mixture with the prawns. Season to taste.

4 Whisk the egg whites until stiff, but not dry, and gently fold them into the fish mixture. When smoothly blended, spoon into a greased gratin dish.

5 Sprinkle with the cheese and bake in a preheated oven at 220°C/425°F/Gas 7 for about 25–30 minutes, until the top is golden and just about firm to the touch. (If it browns too quickly, reduce the oven temperature to 200°C/400°F/Gas 6.)

Roast Sea Bass

Sea bass has quite meaty flesh. It is an expensive fish, best cooked as simply as possible. Avoid elaborate sauces, which would mask its delicate flavour.

INGREDIENTS

Serves 4

1 fennel bulb with fronds, about
 275g/10oz

2 lemons, cut in half

120ml/4fl oz/½ cup olive oil

1 small red onion, diced

2 sea bass, about 500g/1¼lb each, cleaned
 with heads left on

120ml/4fl oz/½ cup dry white wine

salt and freshly ground black pepper

1 Preheat the oven to 190°C/ 375°F/Gas 5. Cut the fronds and green stalks off the top of the fennel and reserve. Cut the fennel bulb lengthways into thin wedges, then into dice. Cut one half lemon into four slices. Squeeze the juice from the remaining lemon halves.

2 Heat 30ml/2 tbsp of the oil in a frying pan and sauté the fennel and onion, stirring frequently, for about 5 minutes, until softened. Remove from the heat.

3 Make three deep cuts in each side of the fish. Place in an oiled roasting tin with the fennel stalks, and tuck 2 lemon slices inside each fish. Scatter over the sautéd fennel and onion.

4 Whisk together the remaining oil, the lemon juice and seasoning and pour over the fish. Cover with foil and roast for 30 minutes, removing the foil for the last 10 minutes. Remove the lemon slices and transfer the fish to a heated serving platter.

5 Set the roasting tin over a medium heat. Add the wine and stir to incorporate all the pan juices. Bring to the boil, then spoon the juices over the fish. Garnish with the fennel fronds and lemon slices and serve.

Whole Cooked Salmon

*Farmed salmon has made this fish
more affordable and less of a treat,
but a whole salmon still features as
a centrepiece at parties. It is never
served with cold meats, but is
usually accompanied by salads and
mayonnaise. As with all fish, the
taste depends on freshness and on
not overcooking it, so although you
need to start the preparation early,
the cooking time is short.*

INGREDIENTS

Serves about 10 as part of a buffet

2–3kg/5–6lb fresh whole salmon

30ml/2 tbsp oil

1 lemon

salt and freshly ground black pepper

lemon wedges, cucumber and fresh dill
   sprigs, to garnish

1 Wash the salmon and dry it
well, inside and out. Pour half
the oil on to a large piece of strong
foil and place the fish in the centre.

2 Put a few slices of lemon inside
the salmon and arrange some
more on the top. Season well and
sprinkle over the remaining oil.
Wrap up the foil to make a loose
parcel. Put the parcel on another
sheet of foil or a baking sheet and
cook in a preheated oven at 200°C/
400°F/Gas 6 for 10 minutes. Turn
off the oven, do not open the door
and leave for several hours.

3 To serve the same day, remove
the foil and peel off the skin. If
you are keeping it for the following
day, leave the skin on and chill the
fish overnight. Arrange the fish on
a large platter and garnish with
lemon wedges, cucumber cut into
thin ribbons and sprigs of dill.

Prawn Soufflé

This makes a very elegant lunch dish and is simple to prepare.

Serves 4–6

25g/1oz butter, plus extra for greasing

15ml/1 tbsp fine dried white breadcrumbs

175g/6oz cooked peeled prawns, deveined and coarsely chopped

15ml/1 tbsp finely chopped fresh tarragon or parsley

45ml/3 tbsp sherry or dry white wine

freshly ground black pepper

lemon slices, whole prawn and flat leaf parsley sprig, to garnish

For the soufflé mixture

40g/1½oz butter

37.5ml/2½ tbsp plain flour

250ml/8fl oz/1 cup milk, heated

4 eggs, separated, plus 1 egg white

salt

1 Butter a 1.5–1.75 litre/2½–3 pint/6¼–7½ cup soufflé dish. Sprinkle with the breadcrumbs, tilting the dish to coat the bottom and sides evenly.

2 Melt the butter in a small saucepan. Add the chopped prawns and cook for 2–3 minutes over a low heat. Stir in the tarragon or parsley and sherry or wine and season with pepper. Cook for a further 1–2 minutes. Raise the heat and boil rapidly to evaporate the liquid, then remove from the heat and set aside.

3 To make the soufflé mixture, melt the butter in a heavy-based saucepan. Add the flour, blending well with a wire whisk. Cook over a low heat for 2–3 minutes. Pour in the hot milk and whisk vigorously until smooth. Simmer for 2 minutes, still whisking, then season to taste with salt.

4 Remove the pan from the heat and immediately beat in the egg yolks, 1 at a time. Stir in the prawn mixture.

5 Whisk the egg whites in a large bowl until they form stiff peaks. Stir about one-quarter of the egg whites into the prawn mixture, then gently fold in the rest of the egg whites.

6 Carefully turn the mixture into the prepared dish. Bake in a preheated oven at 190°C/375°F/Gas 5 for about 30–40 minutes, until the soufflé is puffed up and light golden brown on top. Serve at once, with lemon slices, a whole prawn and a parsley sprig garnish.

VARIATIONS

For lobster soufflé, substitute 1 large lobster tail for the cooked prawns. Chop it finely and add to the saucepan with the herbs and wine in place of the prawns. For crab soufflé, instead of prawns, use about 175g/6oz fresh crab meat or a 200g/7oz can, drained. Flake and pick over carefully to remove any bits of shell.

Crab with Spring Onions and Ginger

This recipe is far less complicated to make than it first appears. Buy live crabs, if you can, for the best flavour and texture.

Serves 4

1 large or 2 medium crabs, weighing about 675g/1½lb in total

30ml/2 tbsp Chinese rice wine or dry sherry

1 egg, lightly beaten

15ml/1 tbsp cornflour paste

45–60ml/3–4 tbsp vegetable oil

15ml/1 tbsp finely chopped fresh root ginger

3–4 spring onions, cut into short sections

30ml/2 tbsp light soy sauce

5ml/1 tsp soft light brown sugar

about 75ml/5 tbsp vegetable or chicken stock

few drops sesame oil

shredded spring onion, to garnish

stir-fried noodles, to serve

3 Heat the oil in a preheated wok and stir-fry the crab pieces, together with the chopped ginger and spring onions, for about 2–3 minutes.

4 Add the soy sauce, sugar and stock and blend well. Bring to the boil, cover and braise for 3–4 minutes. Sprinkle with sesame oil, garnish with spring onion and serve with stir-fried noodles.

1 Cut the crab in half from the underbelly. Break off the claws and crack them with the back of a cleaver. Discard the legs and crack the shell, breaking it into several pieces. Discard the feathery gills and the sac.

2 Put the crab pieces in a bowl. Mix together the rice wine or sherry, egg and cornflour paste, pour over the crab and set aside to marinate for 10–15 minutes.

Seafood in Puff Pastry

This classic combination of seafood in a creamy sauce served in a puff pastry case is found as an hors d'oeuvre on the menus of many elegant restaurants in France.

INGREDIENTS

Serves 6

butter, for greasing

350g/12oz rough puff or puff pastry

1 egg beaten with 15ml/1 tbsp water, to glaze

60ml/4 tbsp dry white wine

2 shallots, finely chopped

450g/1lb mussels, scrubbed and 'debearded'

15g/½oz/1 tbsp butter

450g/1lb shelled scallops, cut in half crossways

450g/1lb raw prawns, peeled and deveined

175g/6oz cooked lobster meat, sliced

For the sauce

225g/8oz unsalted butter, diced

2 shallots, finely chopped

250ml/8fl oz/1 cup fish stock

90ml/6 tbsp dry white wine

15–30ml/1–2 tbsp double cream

lemon juice

salt and freshly ground white pepper

fresh dill sprigs, to garnish

1 Lightly grease a large baking sheet and sprinkle with a little water. On a lightly floured surface, roll out the pastry into a rectangle slightly less than 5mm/¼in thick. Using a sharp knife, cut into 6 diamond shapes about 13cm/5in long. Transfer to the baking sheet. Brush the pastry with the egg glaze. Using the tip of a knife, score a line 1cm/½in from the edge, then lightly mark the centre in a criss-cross pattern.

2 Chill the pastry cases for 30 minutes. Bake in a preheated oven at 220°C/425°F/Gas 7 for about 20 minutes, until puffed and brown. Transfer to a wire rack and, while still hot, remove each lid, cutting along the scored line to free it. Scoop out any uncooked dough from the bases and discard, then leave the cases to cool completely.

3 In a large saucepan, bring the wine and shallots to the boil over a high heat. Add the mussels to the pan, cover tightly and cook, shaking the pan occasionally, for 4–6 minutes, until the shells open. Remove any mussels that do not open. Reserve 6 mussels for the garnish, then remove the rest from their shells and set aside in a bowl, covered. Strain the cooking liquid through a muslin-lined sieve and reserve for the sauce.

4 In a heavy frying pan, melt the butter over a medium heat. Add the scallops and prawns, cover tightly and cook for 3–4 minutes, shaking and stirring occasionally, until they feel just firm to the touch; do not overcook.

5 Using a slotted spoon, transfer the scallops and prawns to the bowl with the mussels and add any cooking juices to the reserved mussel cooking liquid.

6 To make the sauce, melt 25g/1oz of the butter in a heavy saucepan. Add the shallots and cook for 2 minutes. Pour in the fish stock and boil for about 15 minutes over a high heat, until reduced by three-quarters. Add the white wine and reserved cooking liquid and boil for 5–7 minutes, until reduced by half. Lower the heat to medium and whisk in the remaining butter, a little at a time, to make a smooth thick sauce (lift the pan from the heat if the sauce begins to boil). Whisk in the cream and season with salt, if needed, pepper and lemon juice. Keep the sauce warm over a very low heat, stirring frequently.

7 Warm the pastry cases in a low oven for about 10 minutes. Put the mussels, scallops and prawns in a large saucepan. Stir in a quarter of the sauce and reheat gently over a low heat. Gently stir in the lobster meat and cook for 1 further minute.

8 Arrange the pastry case bases on individual plates. Divide the seafood mixture equally among them and top with the lids. Garnish each with a mussel in its half-shell and a dill sprig and spoon the remaining sauce around the edges or serve separately.

FRIED &
GRILLED DISHES

~

Pan-fried Sole with Lemon

The delicate flavour and texture of sole can be enjoyed to the full in this simple, classic recipe. Lemon sole is used here because it is easier to obtain – and less expensive – than Dover sole.

INGREDIENTS

Serves 2

30–45ml/2–3 tbsp plain flour

4 lemon sole fillets

45ml/3 tbsp olive oil

50g/2oz/¼ cup butter

60ml/4 tbsp lemon juice

30ml/2 tbsp bottled capers, drained
   and rinsed

salt and freshly ground black pepper

fresh flat leaf parsley and lemon wedges,
   to garnish

1 Season the flour with salt and black pepper. Coat the lemon sole fillets with the seasoned flour evenly on both sides, shaking off any excess. Heat the olive oil with half the butter in a large shallow saucepan or frying pan until foaming. Add two of the lemon sole fillets and fry over a medium heat for about 2–3 minutes on each side, until golden.

2 Carefully lift out the sole fillets with a fish slice and place them on a warmed serving platter. Cover with foil and keep hot. Fry the remaining sole fillets in the same way and transfer them to the serving platter.

3 Remove the pan from the heat and stir in the lemon juice and the remaining butter. Return the pan to a high heat and stir vigorously until the butter is fully incorporated and the pan juices are sizzling and beginning to turn golden brown. Remove from the heat and stir in the capers.

4 Pour the pan juices over the sole, sprinkle with salt and pepper to taste and garnish with the parsley. Add the lemon wedges and serve at once.

COOK'S TIP

It is important to cook the pan juices to the right colour after removing the fish. Too pale, and they will taste insipid; too dark, and they may taste bitter. Take great care not to be distracted at this point so that you can watch the colour of the juices change to a golden brown.

Herrings in Oatmeal with Mustard

Oatmeal makes a delicious, crunchy coating for tender herrings.

INGREDIENTS

Serves 4

about 15ml/1 tbsp Dijon mustard

about 7.5ml/1½ tsp tarragon vinegar

175ml/6fl oz/¾ cup thick mayonnaise

4 herrings, about 225g/8oz each, gutted
and cleaned

1 lemon, halved

115g/4oz medium oatmeal

salt and freshly ground black pepper

1 Beat mustard and vinegar to taste into the mayonnaise. Chill lightly.

2 Place one fish at a time on a board, cut side down and opened out. Press gently along the backbone with your thumbs. Turn over the fish and carefully lift away the backbone.

3 Squeeze lemon juice over both sides of the fish, then season with salt and pepper. Fold the fish in half, skin side outwards.

4 Place the oatmeal on a plate, then coat each herring evenly in the oatmeal, pressing it in gently but firmly.

5 Place the herrings on a grill rack and cook under a preheated moderately hot grill for 3–4 minutes on each side, until the skin is golden brown and crisp and the flesh flakes easily. Serve immediately with the mustard sauce, served separately.

Fish and Chips

This classic British dish is quick and easy to make at home.

INGREDIENTS

Serves 4

115g/4oz self-raising flour

150ml/¼ pint/⅔ cup water

675g/1½lb potatoes

675g/1½lb piece skinned cod fillet, cut
into 4 pieces

oil, for deep-frying

salt

lemon wedges, to garnish

1 Sift the flour and a pinch of salt together in a bowl, then form a well in the centre. Gradually pour in the water, whisking in the flour to make a smooth batter. Set aside to rest for 30 minutes.

2 Cut the potatoes into strips about 1cm/½in wide and 5cm/2 in long. Place them in a colander and rinse in cold water, then drain and dry well.

3 Heat the oil in a deep-fat fryer or large heavy pan to 150°C/ 300°F. Using the wire basket, lower the potatoes in batches into the oil and cook for 5–6 minutes, shaking the basket occasionally until the potatoes are soft but not browned. Remove the chips from the oil and drain thoroughly on kitchen paper.

4 Heat the oil in the fryer to 190°C/375°F. Season the fish. Stir the batter, then dip the pieces of fish into it, in turn, allowing the excess to drain off.

5 Working in two batches if necessary, lower the fish into the oil and fry for 6–8 minutes, until crisp and golden brown. Drain the fish on kitchen paper and keep warm.

6 Add the chips in batches to the oil and cook for 2–3 minutes, until golden brown and crisp. Keep hot. Sprinkle with salt and serve with the fish, garnished with lemon wedges.

Fish Steaks with Coriander-lime Butter

Citrus-flavoured butter adds just the right kind of zip to fish steaks.

INGREDIENTS

Serves 4

675g/1½lb swordfish or tuna steak,
   2.5cm/1in thick, cut into 4 pieces
60ml/4 tbsp vegetable oil
30ml/2 tbsp lemon juice
15ml/1 tbsp lime juice
salt and freshly ground black pepper
coriander-lime butter (see Cook's Tip)
asparagus and lime slices, to serve

1 Put the fish steaks in a shallow dish. Combine the oil, lemon juice and lime juice, season and pour over the fish. Cover and refrigerate for 1–2 hours, turning the fish once or twice.

2 Drain the fish steaks and arrange on the rack in the grill pan or set over the hot charcoal about 13cm/5in from the coals. Grill for 3–4 minutes, or until the fish is just firm to the touch but still moist in the centre, turning the steaks over once.

3 Transfer to warmed plates and top each fish steak with a pat of coriander-lime butter. Serve the fish immediately with asparagus and slices of lime.

COOK'S TIP

For coriander-lime butter, finely chop 25g/1oz fresh coriander. Mix into 115g/4oz softened, unsalted butter, together with the grated rind and juice of 1 lime. Roll the butter neatly in greaseproof paper and chill in the refrigerator until firm. Other flavoured butters can be made in the same way. Try parsley-lemon butter, made from 30ml/2 tbsp chopped parsley, 115g/4oz unsalted butter and 15ml/1 tbsp lemon juice.

Turkish Cold Fish

Cold fish dishes are appreciated in the Middle East and for good reason – they are delicious! This particular version from Turkey can be made using mackerel, if preferred.

INGREDIENTS

Serves 4

60ml/4 tbsp olive oil

900g/2lb porgy or snapper

2 onions, sliced

1 green pepper, seeded and sliced

1 red pepper, seeded and sliced

3 garlic cloves, crushed

15ml/1 tbsp tomato purée

50ml/2fl oz/¼ cup fish stock, bottled clam
    juice or water

5–6 tomatoes, skinned and sliced or
    400g/14oz can tomatoes

30ml/2 tbsp chopped fresh parsley

30ml/2 tbsp lemon juice

5ml/1 tsp paprika

15–20 green and black olives

salt and freshly ground black pepper

bread and salad, to serve

1 Heat 30ml/2 tbsp of the oil in a large roasting tin or frying pan and fry the fish on both sides until golden brown. Remove from the tin or pan, cover and keep warm.

2 Heat the remaining oil in the pan and fry the onion for 2–3 minutes until softened. Add the peppers and continue cooking for 3–4 minutes, stirring occasionally, then add the garlic and stir-fry for 1 more minute.

3 Blend the tomato purée with the fish stock, clam juice or water and stir into the pan with the tomatoes, parsley, lemon juice, paprika and seasoning. Simmer very gently for 15 minutes, stirring occasionally.

4 Return the fish to the pan and cover with the sauce. Cook for 10 minutes, then add the olives and cook for a further 5 minutes or until just cooked through.

5 Transfer the fish to a serving dish and pour the sauce over the top. Allow to cool, then cover and chill until completely cold. Serve cold with bread and salad.

COOK'S TIP

One large fish looks spectacular, but it is tricky both to cook and to serve. If you prefer, buy 4 smaller fish and cook for a shorter time, until just tender and cooked through.

Salmon Cakes with Spicy Mayonnaise

Taste the difference between home-made fish cakes and the inferior store-bought variety with this delicious recipe.

Serves 4

2 boiling potatoes, about 350g/12oz

350g/12oz salmon fillet, skinned and
   finely chopped

30–45ml/2–3 tbsp chopped fresh dill

15ml/1 tbsp lemon juice

flour for coating

45ml/3 tbsp vegetable oil

salt and freshly ground black pepper

spicy mayonnaise (see Cook's Tip) and
   salad leaves, to serve

1 Put the potatoes in a saucepan of boiling salted water and parboil them for 15 minutes.

2 Meanwhile, combine the salmon, dill, lemon juice, salt and pepper in a large bowl.

3 Drain the potatoes and leave them to cool. When they are cool enough to handle, peel away the skins.

4 Shred the potatoes into strips on the coarse side of a grater.

5 Add to the salmon mixture. Mix gently together with your fingers, breaking up the strips of potato as little as possible.

6 Divide the salmon and potato mixture into 8 portions. Shape each into a compact cake, pressing well together. Flatten the cakes to about 1cm/½in thickness.

7 Coat the salmon cakes lightly with flour, shaking off excess.

8 Heat the oil in a large frying pan. Add the salmon cakes and fry for 5 minutes or until crisp and golden brown on both sides.

9 Drain the salmon cakes on kitchen paper and serve with the spicy mayonnaise and salad.

COOK'S TIP

To make spicy mayonnaise, mix together 350ml/12fl oz/1½ cups mayonnaise, 10ml/2 tsp Dijon mustard, 2.5–5ml/½–1 tsp Worcestershire sauce and a dash of Tabasco sauce. You can use home-made or good quality commercial mayonnaise.

Whiting Fillets in a Polenta Crust

Polenta is sometimes called cornmeal. Use quick and easy polenta if you can, as it will give a better crunchy coating.

Serves 4

8 small whiting fillets

finely grated rind of 1 lemon

225g/8oz polenta

30ml/2 tbsp olive oil

15ml/1 tbsp butter

30ml/2 tbsp mixed fresh herbs, such as parsley, chervil and chives

salt and freshly ground black pepper

toasted pine nuts and red onion, sliced, to garnish

steamed spinach, to serve

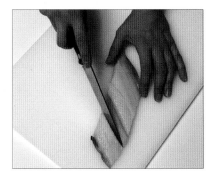

1 Make 4 small cuts in each fillet to stop the fish curling up when it is cooked.

2 Sprinkle the seasoning and lemon rind over the fish.

3 Press the polenta on to the fillets. Chill in the refrigerator for 30 minutes.

4 Heat the oil and butter in a large frying pan and gently fry the fillets on each side for 3–4 minutes. Sprinkle over the fresh herbs and garnish with toasted pine nuts and red onion slices. Serve immediately with steamed spinach.

Monkfish with Peppered Citrus Marinade

Monkfish is a firm, meaty fish that cooks well on the barbecue and keeps its shape.

INGREDIENTS

Serves 4

2 monkfish tails, about 350g/12oz each

1 lime

1 lemon

2 oranges

handful of fresh thyme sprigs

30ml/2 tbsp olive oil

15ml/1 tbsp mixed peppercorns, roughly crushed

salt and freshly ground black pepper

lemon and lime wedges, to serve

1 Remove any skin from the monkfish tails. Cut carefully down one side of the backbone, sliding the knife between the bone and flesh, to remove the fillet on one side. You can ask your fishmonger to do this for you.

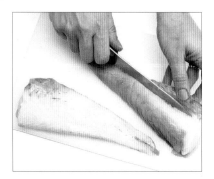

2 Turn the fish and repeat on the other side, to remove the second fillet. Repeat on the second tail. Lay the 4 fillets out flat.

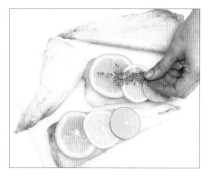

3 Cut 2 slices each from the lime, lemon and 1 orange and arrange them over 2 of the fillets. Add a few sprigs of thyme and sprinkle with salt and pepper. Finely grate the rind from the remaining fruit and sprinkle it over the fish.

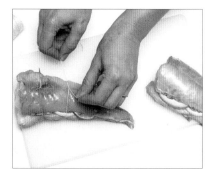

4 Lay the remaining 2 fish fillets on top and tie them firmly with fine cotton string to hold them in shape. Arrange them in a wide dish.

5 Squeeze the juice from the remaining lime, lemon and oranges and mix it with the oil and more salt and pepper. Spoon over the fish. Cover and leave to marinate for about 1 hour, turning occasionally and spooning the marinade over it.

6 Drain the monkfish, reserving the marinade, and sprinkle with the crushed peppercorns. Cook on a medium-hot barbecue for 15–20 minutes, basting it with the marinade and turning it occasionally, until it is evenly cooked through. Serve with lemon and lime wedges.

VARIATION

You can also use this marinade for monkfish kebabs.

Fish Fillets with Orange and Tomato Sauce

Citrus flavours liven up any plain white fish beautifully.

INGREDIENTS

Serves 4

45ml/3 tbsp plain flour

4 fillets of firm white fish, such as cod, sea bass or sole, about 675g/1½lb

15g/½oz butter or margarine

30ml/2 tbsp olive oil

1 onion, sliced

2 garlic cloves, chopped

1.5ml/¼ tsp ground cumin

500g/1¼lb tomatoes, skinned, seeded and chopped, or 400g/14oz canned chopped tomatoes

120ml/4fl oz/½ cup fresh orange juice

salt and freshly ground black pepper

orange wedges, for garnishing

1 Put the flour on a plate and season well with salt and pepper. Coat the fish fillets lightly with the seasoned flour, shaking off any excess.

2 Heat the butter or margarine and half the oil in a large frying pan. Add the fish fillets to the pan and cook for about 3 minutes on each side, until golden brown and the flesh flakes easily when tested with a fork.

3 When the fish is cooked, transfer to a warmed serving platter. Cover with foil and keep warm while you make the sauce.

4 Heat the remaining oil in the pan. Add the onion and garlic and cook for about 5 minutes, until softened but not coloured.

5 Stir in the ground cumin, tomatoes and orange juice. Bring to the boil and cook, stirring frequently, for about 10 minutes, until thickened.

6 Garnish the fish with orange wedges and serve immediately, passing the sauce separately.

Cajun-style Cod

*This recipe works equally well with
any firm-fleshed fish, such as
swordfish, shark, tuna or halibut.*

INGREDIENTS

Serves 4

4 cod steaks, each weighing about
    175g/6oz
30ml/2 tbsp plain yogurt
15ml/1 tbsp lime or lemon juice
1 garlic clove, crushed
5ml/1 tsp ground cumin
5ml/1 tsp paprika
5ml/1 tsp mustard powder
2.5ml/½ tsp cayenne powder
2.5ml/½ tsp dried thyme
2.5ml/½ tsp oregano
vegetable oil, for brushing
baby potatoes and mixed salad, to serve

1 Pat the fish dry on absorbent
kitchen paper. Mix together
the yogurt and lime or lemon juice
and brush lightly over both sides
of the fish.

2 Mix together the garlic, cumin,
paprika, mustard powder,
cayenne, thyme and oregano. Coat
both sides of the fish with the
seasoning mix, rubbing in well.

3 Brush a ridged grill pan or
heavy-based frying pan with a
little oil. Heat until very hot. Add
the fish and cook over a high heat
for 4 minutes, or until the
underside is well browned.

4 Brush the fish with a little
more oil, if necessary, turn
over and cook for a further
4 minutes, or until the steaks have
cooked through. Serve at once,
accompanied with baby potatoes
and a mixed salad.

Marinated Fish

This dish is of Spanish origin and is also very popular throughout the Caribbean.

Serves 4–6

7.5ml/1½ tsp garlic granules

2.5ml/½ tsp coarse-grain black pepper

2.5ml/½ tsp paprika

2.5ml/½ tsp celery salt

2.5 ml/½ tsp curry powder

900g/2lb cod fillet

½ lemon

15ml/1 tbsp spice seasoning

flour, for dusting

oil, for frying

lemon wedges, to garnish

For the sauce

30ml/2 tbsp vegetable oil

1 onion, sliced

½ red pepper, sliced

½ christophene or chayote, peeled and
    seeded, cut into small pieces

2 garlic cloves, crushed

120ml/4fl oz/½ cup malt vinegar

75ml/5 tbsp water

2.5ml/½ tsp ground allspice

1 bay leaf

1 small hot pepper, chopped

15ml/1 tbsp soft dark brown sugar

salt and freshly ground black pepper

1 Mix together all the spices. Place the fish in a shallow dish, squeeze over the lemon, then sprinkle with the spice seasoning and pat into the fish. Leave to marinate in a cool place for 1 hour.

2 Cut the fish into 7.5cm/3in pieces and dust with a little flour, shaking off the excess.

3 Heat the oil in a heavy frying pan and fry the fish pieces for 2–3 minutes until golden brown and crisp, turning occasionally.

4 To make the sauce, heat the oil in a heavy frying pan and fry the onion until soft. Add the pepper, christophene or chayote and garlic and stir-fry for 2 minutes. Pour in the vinegar, add the remaining ingredients and simmer gently for 5 minutes. Leave to stand for 10 minutes, then pour over the fish. Serve hot, garnished with lemon wedges.

Lobster Thermidor

*Lobster Thermidor takes its name
from the eleventh month of the
French Revolutionary calendar,
which falls in midsummer, although
this rich dish is equally delicious in
colder weather, too. Serve one lobster
per person as a main course or one
filled shell each for a starter.*

INGREDIENTS

Serves 2–4

2 live lobsters, about 675g/1½lb each

20g/¾oz/1½ tbsp butter

30ml/2 tbsp plain flour

30ml/2 tbsp brandy

120ml/4fl oz/½ cup milk

90ml/6 tbsp whipping cream

15ml/1 tbsp Dijon mustard

lemon juice

salt and freshly ground white pepper

grated Parmesan cheese,
    for sprinkling

fresh parsley and dill, to garnish

1 Bring a large saucepan of
lightly salted water to the boil.
Plunge the lobsters into the pan
head first and cook for about
8–10 minutes.

2 Remove the lobsters from
the pan, cut them in half
lengthways and discard the dark
sac behind the eyes, then pull out
the string-like intestine from the
tail. Remove the meat from the
shells, reserving the coral and liver,
then rinse the shells and wipe dry.
Cut the meat into bite-size pieces.

3 Melt the butter in a heavy-
based saucepan over a medium
heat. Add the flour and cook,
stirring constantly, until it is just
turning golden. Pour in the brandy
and milk, whisking vigorously
until smooth, then whisk in the
cream and mustard.

4 Press the lobster coral and liver
through a strainer into the
sauce and whisk to blend. Reduce
the heat to low and simmer gently,
stirring frequently, for about
10 minutes, until thickened.
Season with salt, if necessary,
pepper and lemon juice.

5 Preheat the grill. Arrange the
lobster shells in a gratin dish
or shallow flameproof dish.

6 Stir the lobster meat into the
sauce and divide the mixture
between the shells. Sprinkle with
Parmesan and grill until golden.
Serve garnished with herbs.

Cauliflower, Prawn and Broccoli Tempura

All sorts of vegetables are delicious deep fried in this Japanese style. Firm vegetables, such as cauliflower and broccoli, are best blanched before frying but mangetout, slices of red and green pepper, and mushrooms can simply be dipped in the batter and fried.

INGREDIENTS

Serves 4

½ cauliflower

275g/10oz broccoli

8 raw prawns

sunflower or vegetable oil,
    for deep-frying

8 button mushrooms (optional)

lemon wedges and sprigs of coriander,
    to garnish (optional)

soy sauce, to serve

For the batter

115g/4oz/1 cup plain flour

pinch of salt

2 eggs, separated

175ml/6fl oz/¾ cup iced water

30ml/2 tbsp sunflower or vegetable oil

1 Cut the cauliflower and broccoli into medium-size florets. Blanch all the florets for 1–2 minutes. Drain, refresh under cold running water and set aside. Peel the prawns, but leave their tails intact, and set aside.

COOK'S TIP

Try cooking other vegetables in this way, such as aubergines and courgettes, or even celery leaves.

2 To make the batter, place the flour and salt in a bowl. Blend together the egg yolks and water and stir into the flour, beating well to make a smooth batter.

3 Beat in the oil. Whisk the egg whites until stiff and then fold them into the batter. Heat the oil for deep-frying to 190°C/375°F. Coat a few of the vegetables and prawns in the batter.

4 Fry for about 2–3 minutes, until lightly golden and puffy. Transfer to a plate lined with kitchen paper and keep warm while you are frying the remaining prawns and vegetables.

5 Arrange the tempura on individual serving plates, garnish with wedges of lemon and coriander sprigs, if liked, and serve with little bowls of soy sauce.

King Prawns with Vermouth

The delicate herb flavouring in French vermouth perfectly offsets this delightful Mediterranean-style prawn dish.

Serves 4

20 raw king prawns

½ cucumber

25g/1oz/2 tbsp butter

15ml/1 tbsp olive oil

1 small shallot, finely chopped

25g/1oz/¼ cup drained sun-dried
    tomatoes in oil, chopped

60ml/4 tbsp vegetable stock

30ml/2 tbsp vermouth

150ml/¼ pint/⅔ cup double cream

15ml/1 tbsp chopped fennel leaves

45ml/3 tbsp golden salmon roe

salt and freshly ground
    white pepper

fennel leaves, to garnish

1 Remove the heads from the prawns. If you prefer, you could also peel them, in which case cut each prawn down the back and remove the black vein.

2 Peel the cucumber, cut it in half lengthways and then scoop out the seeds. Slice the cucumber thickly into crescents.

3 Heat the butter and oil together in a large frying pan, add the chopped shallot and fry over a medium heat, stirring frequently, until softened.

4 Add the tomatoes, stock, vermouth and prawns. Cook over a low heat for 8–10 minutes.

5 Cook the cucumber crescents in a small pan of boiling salted water for 3 minutes, then drain.

6 Stir the cream and chopped fennel leaves into the prawns and cook until the sauce thickens. Season to taste and stir in the cooked cucumber and the salmon roe. Reheat and serve, garnished with fennel leaves.

COOK'S TIP

Try using sun-dried peppers instead of the tomatoes. The salmon roe adds a delicious flavour, but it is not essential.

CASSEROLES
& STEWS

~

Green Fish Curry

This dish combines all the typical flavours of the East.

INGREDIENTS

Serves 4

1.5ml/¼ tsp ground turmeric

30ml/2 tbsp lime juice

4 cod fillets, skinned and cut into
    5cm/2in chunks

1 onion, chopped

1 fresh large green chilli, roughly
    chopped

1 garlic clove, crushed

25g/1oz cashew nuts

2.5ml/½ tsp fennel seeds

30ml/2 tbsp desiccated coconut

30ml/2 tbsp oil

1.5ml/¼ tsp cumin seeds

1.5ml/¼ tsp ground coriander

1.5ml/¼ tsp ground cumin

150ml/¼ pint/⅔ cup water

175ml/6fl oz/¾ cup single cream

45ml/3 tbsp finely chopped
    fresh coriander

salt

fresh coriander sprig, to garnish

vegetable pilau, to serve (optional)

1 Mix together the turmeric, lime juice and a pinch of salt and rub over the fish. Cover and leave to marinate for 15 minutes.

2 Meanwhile work the onion, chilli, garlic, cashew nuts, fennel seeds and coconut to a paste in a food processor or in a mortar with a pestle. Spoon the paste into a bowl and set aside.

3 Heat the oil in a large frying pan and fry the cumin seeds for 2 minutes, until they begin to splutter. Add the spice paste and fry for 5 minutes, then stir in the ground coriander, cumin and water. Fry, stirring frequently, for about 2–3 minutes.

4 Add the single cream and the fresh coriander. Simmer for 5 minutes. Add the fish and gently stir in. Cover and cook gently for 10 minutes, until the fish is tender. Garnish with a coriander sprig and serve with vegetable pilau, if liked.

Creole Fish Stew

A simple, attractive dish – good for an informal dinner party.

INGREDIENTS

Serves 4–6

2 whole red bream or large snapper, cleaned and cut into 2.5cm/1in pieces
30ml/2 tbsp spice seasoning
30ml/2 tbsp malt vinegar
flour, for dusting
oil, for frying

For the sauce
30ml/2 tbsp vegetable oil
15g/½oz butter or margarine
1 onion, finely chopped
275g/10oz fresh tomatoes, skinned and finely chopped
2 garlic cloves, crushed
2 thyme sprigs
600ml/1 pint/2½ cups fish stock or water
2.5ml/½ tsp ground cinnamon
1 hot chilli, chopped
115g/4oz red pepper, finely chopped
115g/4oz green pepper, finely chopped
salt
oregano sprigs, to garnish

1 Sprinkle the fish with the spice seasoning and vinegar, turning to coat. Set aside in the refrigerator to marinate for a minimum of 2 hours or overnight.

2 When ready to cook, place a little flour on a large plate and coat the fish pieces, shaking off any excess flour.

3 Heat a little oil in a large frying pan and fry the fish pieces for about 5 minutes, until golden brown, then set aside. Do not worry if the fish is not cooked through, it will finish cooking in the sauce.

4 To make the sauce, heat the oil and butter or margarine in a large frying pan or wok and stir-fry the onion for 5 minutes. Add the tomatoes, garlic and thyme, stir well and simmer for a further 5 minutes. Stir in the stock or water, cinnamon and hot chilli.

5 Add the fish pieces and the chopped red and green peppers. Simmer until the fish is cooked through and the stock has reduced to a thick sauce. Adjust the seasoning with salt. Serve hot, garnished with oregano.

Italian Fish Stew

Italians are renowned for enjoying good food, especially if it is shared with all the members of an extended family. This stew is a veritable feast of fish and seafood in a delicious tomato broth, suitable for a more modest family lunch.

INGREDIENTS

Serves 4

30ml/2 tbsp olive oil

1 onion, thinly sliced

a few saffron threads

5ml/1 tsp dried thyme

large pinch of cayenne pepper

2 garlic cloves, finely chopped

2 x 400g/14oz cans peeled tomatoes, drained and chopped

175ml/6fl oz/¾ cup dry white wine

2 litres/3¼ pints/8 cups hot fish stock

350g/12oz white, skinless fish fillets, cut into pieces

450g/1lb monkfish, membrane removed, cut into pieces

450g/1lb mussels in the shell, scrubbed and 'beards' removed

225g/8oz small squid, cleaned and cut into rings

30ml/2 tbsp chopped fresh basil or parsley

salt and freshly ground black pepper

thickly sliced bread, to serve

1 Heat the oil in a large, heavy-based saucepan. Add the onion, saffron, thyme, cayenne pepper and salt, to taste. Stir well and cook over a low heat for about 8–10 minutes, until the onion is soft. Add the garlic and cook for a further 1 minute.

2 Stir in the tomatoes, wine and fish stock. Bring to the boil and boil for 1 minute, then reduce the heat and simmer gently for 15 minutes.

3 Add the white fish fillet and monkfish pieces to the pan and simmer gently over a low heat for a further 3 minutes.

4 Add the mussels and squid rings and simmer for about 2 minutes, until the mussels open. Discard any that remain closed. Stir in the basil or parsley and season to taste. Ladle into warmed soup bowls and serve with bread.

French Fish Stew

A traditional recipe using freshwater fish cooked in red wine and brandy; an ideal dish for entertaining.

INGREDIENTS

Serves 6

1.5kg/3–3½lb freshwater fish, such as carp,
    trout and skinned eel
45ml/3 tbsp plain flour
50g/2oz/4 tbsp butter
225g/8oz smoked bacon, cut
    into lardons
4 shallots, very finely chopped
225g/8oz small onions
225g/8oz/3 cups mushrooms, chopped
120ml/4fl oz/½ cup brandy
1 litre/1¾ pints/4 cups red wine
300ml/½ pint/1¼ cups veal or
    chicken stock
1 garlic clove, crushed
1 bouquet garni
salt and freshly ground black pepper
chopped fresh parsley, to garnish
garlic bread, to serve

1 Clean the carp and trout, remove the heads and fins, fillet the flesh and cut into slices. Cut the eel into chunks.

2 Put half of the flour into a plastic bag, season with salt and pepper, add the fish pieces and shake to coat.

3 In a large pan, melt the butter over a medium heat. Add the fish pieces and brown them on both sides. Remove the fish from the pan and set aside.

4 Add the lardons, shallots and onions to the pan and cook over a low heat for about 10 minutes, until golden. Stir in the chopped mushrooms and cook for a further 5 minutes.

5 Stir in the brandy and, if you wish to flambé, ignite with a match, shaking the pan until the flames have died down. Add the wine, bring to the boil and simmer for 2–3 minutes.

6 Stir in the veal or chicken stock, garlic and bouquet garni, bring to the boil and simmer over a low heat for 5 minutes. Add the fish and simmer until cooked.

7 With a slotted spoon, remove the fish and keep hot. In a small bowl, blend the remaining flour with a little cold water and stir into the pan. Bring to the boil and cook for 5 minutes, then return the fish to the pan. Serve garnished with chopped parsley and accompanied by garlic bread.

COOK'S TIP

If carp is not available, use extra trout, or substitute another fish, such as red mullet, John Dory, monkfish or bream.

Fish Stew with Calvados, Parsley and Dill

This rustic stew harbours all sorts of interesting flavours and will please and intrigue. Many varieties of fish can be used, just choose the freshest and best.

INGREDIENTS

Serves 4

1kg/2¼lb assorted white fish

15ml/1 tbsp chopped fresh parsley, plus a
    few leaves to garnish

225g/8oz mushrooms

225g/8oz can tomatoes

1 large bunch fresh dill sprigs

10ml/2 tsp flour

15g/½oz butter

450ml/¾ pint/1⅞ cups cider

45ml/3 tbsp Calvados

salt and freshly ground black pepper

1 Chop the fish roughly and place it in a casserole or stewing pot with the parsley, mushrooms, tomatoes and salt and pepper to taste. Reserve 4 dill sprigs to garnish and chop the remainder. Add the chopped dill to the casserole.

2 Work the flour into the butter with a fork. Heat the cider and stir in the flour and butter mixture, a little at a time. Cook, stirring, until it has thickened slightly.

3 Add the cider mixture and the Calvados to the fish and mix gently. Cover and bake in a preheated oven at 180°C/350°F/ Gas 4 for about 30 minutes, or until cooked through. Serve at once, garnished with reserved sprigs of dill and the parsley leaves.

Indian Fish Stew

A spicy fish stew made with potatoes, peppers and traditional Indian spices.

INGREDIENTS

Serves 4

30ml/2 tbsp oil

5ml/1 tsp cumin seeds

1 onion, chopped

1 red pepper, thinly sliced

1 garlic clove, crushed

2 red chillies, finely chopped

2 bay leaves

2.5ml/½ tsp salt

5ml/1 tsp ground cumin

5ml/1 tsp ground coriander

5ml/1 tsp chilli powder

400g/14oz can chopped tomatoes

2 large potatoes, cut into 2.5cm/
   1in chunks

300ml/½ pint/1¼ cups fish stock

4 cod fillets

chappatis, to serve

1 Heat the oil in a large deep-sided frying pan and fry the cumin seeds for 2 minutes until they begin to splutter. Add the onion, pepper, garlic, chillies and bay leaves and fry for 5–7 minutes until the onions have browned.

2 Add the salt, ground cumin, ground coriander and chilli powder and cook for 3–4 minutes.

3 Stir in the chopped tomatoes, potatoes and fish stock. Bring to the boil and simmer for a further 10 minutes.

4 Add the fish, then cover and simmer for 10 minutes, or until the fish is tender. Serve with freshly cooked chappatis.

Shellfish with Seasoned Broth

The robust flavour of the shellfish is perfectly offset by a delicate broth infused with fragrant vegetables.

Serves 4

675g/1½lb mussels, scrubbed in cold water
   and debearded
1 small fennel bulb, thinly sliced
1 onion, thinly sliced
1 leek, thinly sliced
1 small carrot, cut in julienne strips
1 garlic clove
1 litre/1¾ pints/4 cups water
pinch of curry powder
pinch of saffron
1 bay leaf
450g/1lb raw large prawns, peeled
   (reserve a few in their shells,
   to garnish)
450g/1lb small shelled scallops
175g/6oz cooked lobster meat,
   sliced (optional)
salt and freshly ground black pepper

1 Put the mussels in a large heavy-based saucepan or flameproof casserole and cover tightly. Cook over a high heat, shaking the pan or casserole occasionally, for 4–6 minutes, until the shells open. When they are cool enough to handle, discard any mussels that have not opened and remove the remainder from their shells. Reserve one or two in their shells to garnish, if liked. Strain the cooking liquid through a muslin-lined strainer and set aside.

2 Put the fennel, onion, leek, carrot and garlic in a large saucepan and add the water, reserved mussel cooking liquid, curry powder, saffron and bay leaf. Bring to the boil and skim off any foam that rises to the surface. Then reduce the heat, cover and simmer gently for 20 minutes, until the vegetables are tender. Remove and discard the garlic clove.

3 Add the prawns, scallops and lobster meat, if using, and simmer for 1 minute. Add the mussels and simmer over a low heat for about 3 minutes, until the scallops have turned opaque and all the shellfish is heated through. Taste and adjust the seasoning, if necessary, then ladle the shellfish and broth into a warm tureen or four shallow soup plates. Garnish with the reserved mussels and prawns and serve immediately.

Crab and Corn Gumbo

Gumbos are traditional Creole dishes, which come from New Orleans, Louisiana, and always contain a roux that gives this dish a distinctly rich flavour.

INGREDIENTS

Serves 4

25g/1oz butter or margarine
25g/1oz plain flour
15ml/1 tbsp vegetable oil
1 onion, finely chopped
115g/4oz okra, trimmed and chopped
2 garlic cloves, crushed
15ml/1 tbsp finely chopped celery
600ml/1 pint/2½ cups fish stock
150ml/¼ pint/⅔ cup sherry
15ml/1 tbsp tomato ketchup
2.5ml/½ tsp dried oregano
1.5ml/¼ tsp mixed spice
10ml/2 tsp Worcestershire sauce
2 corn cobs, sliced
450g/1lb crab claws
cayenne pepper
fresh coriander, to garnish

1 Melt the butter or margarine in a large saucepan over a low heat, add the flour and stir together to make a roux. Cook for about 10 minutes, stirring constantly to prevent burning, while the roux turns golden brown and then darkens to a rich, nutty brown. If black specks appear, the roux must be discarded. Turn the roux on to a plate and set aside.

2 Heat the oil in the same saucepan over a moderate heat, add the onion, okra, garlic and celery and stir to mix together. Cook for a few minutes, then add the stock, sherry, ketchup, oregano, mixed spice, Worcestershire sauce and cayenne pepper to taste.

3 Bring to the boil, then simmer gently for about 10 minutes, until the vegetables are tender. Add the roux, stirring it well into the sauce, and cook for a few minutes, until thickened.

4 Add the corn cobs and crab claws and continue to simmer gently over a low heat for about 10 minutes, until the crab and corn are cooked.

5 Spoon on to warmed serving plates and garnish with sprigs of fresh coriander.

Ragoût of Shellfish with Sweet Scented Basil

Green curry paste is an integral part of Thai cooking and can be used to accompany other dishes made with fish or chicken. Curry pastes will keep for up to 3 weeks stored in an airtight container in the refrigerator.

INGREDIENTS

Serves 4–6

450g/1lb fresh mussels in their shells, scrubbed and with 'beards' removed

60ml/4 tbsp water

225g/8oz medium squid

400ml/14fl oz/1⅔ cups canned coconut milk

300ml/½ pint/1¼ cups chicken or vegetable stock

350g/12oz monkfish, hoki or red snapper, skinned

150g/5oz raw or cooked prawn tails, peeled and deveined

4 scallops, sliced (optional)

75g/3oz French beans, trimmed and cooked

50g/2oz canned bamboo shoots, drained

1 ripe tomato, skinned, seeded, and roughly chopped

4 sprigs large-leaf basil, torn, and strips of fresh red chilli, to garnish

rice, to serve (optional)

For the green curry paste

10ml/2 tsp coriander seeds

2.5ml/½ tsp caraway or cumin seeds

3–4 fresh green chillies, finely chopped

20ml/4 tsp caster sugar

10ml/2 tsp salt

7.5cm/3in piece lemon grass

2cm/¾in piece galingal or fresh root ginger, finely chopped

3 garlic cloves, crushed

4 shallots or 1 medium onion, finely chopped

2cm/¾in square piece shrimp paste

50g/2oz coriander leaves, finely chopped

45ml/3 tbsp fresh mint or basil, finely chopped

2.5ml/½ tsp ground nutmeg

30ml/2 tbsp vegetable oil

1 Place the mussels in a large saucepan, add the water, cover and cook for about 6–8 minutes, until the shells open. Take three-quarters of the mussels out of their shells and set aside. (Discard any which have not opened.) Strain the cooking liquid and set aside.

2 To prepare the squid, trim off the tentacles beneath the eye. Rinse under cold running water, discarding the gut. Remove the 'quill' from inside the body and rub off the paper-thin skin. Cut the body open and score, criss-cross, with a sharp knife. Cut into strips and set aside.

3 To make the green curry paste, dry fry the coriander and caraway or cumin seeds in a wok to release their flavour. Grind the chillies with the sugar and salt in a mortar with a pestle or in a food processor to make a smooth paste. Combine the seeds from the wok with the chillies, add the lemon grass, galingal or ginger, garlic and shallots or onion, then grind or process until smooth.

4 Add the shrimp paste, coriander, mint or basil, nutmeg and vegetable oil. Combine well.

5 Pour the coconut milk into a strainer. Pour the thin part of the milk, together with the chicken or vegetable stock and the reserved mussel cooking liquid, into a wok. Reserve the coconut milk solids. Add 60–75ml/4–5 tbsp of the green curry paste, according to taste. You can add more paste later, if you need to. Boil rapidly until the liquid has reduced completely.

6 Add the coconut milk solids, then add the squid and monkfish, hoki or red snapper. Simmer for 15–20 minutes. Then add the prawns, scallops and cooked mussels with the beans, bamboo shoots and tomato. Simmer for 2–3 minutes, transfer to a bowl and decorate with the basil and chillies. Serve with rice, if you like.

Prawn Curry with Quails' Eggs

Quails' eggs are available from speciality shops and delicatessens. Hens' eggs may be substituted if quails' eggs are hard to find. Use 1 hen's egg to every 4 quails' eggs.

INGREDIENTS

Serves 4

12 quails' eggs

30ml/2 tbsp vegetable oil

4 shallots or 1 medium onion,
    finely chopped

2.5cm/1in piece galingal or fresh root
    ginger, chopped

2 garlic cloves, crushed

5cm/2in piece lemon grass,
    finely shredded

1–2 small, fresh red chillies, seeded and
    finely chopped

2.5ml/½ tsp turmeric

1cm/½ in square piece shrimp paste or
    15ml/1 tbsp fish sauce

900g/2lb raw prawn tails, peeled
    and deveined

400ml/14fl oz/1⅔ cups canned
    coconut milk

300ml/½ pint/1¼ cups chicken stock

115g/4oz Chinese leaves,
    roughly shredded

10ml/2 tsp sugar

2.5ml/½ tsp salt

2 spring onions, green part only,
    shredded, and 30ml/2 tbsp shredded
    coconut, to garnish

1 Cook the quails' eggs in boiling water for 8 minutes. Refresh in cold water, peel and then set aside.

2 Heat the vegetable oil in a large wok, add the shallots or onion, galingal or ginger and garlic and soften without colouring. Add the lemon grass, chillies, turmeric and shrimp paste or fish sauce and fry briefly to bring out their flavours.

3 Add the prawns and fry briefly. Pour the coconut milk through a strainer over a bowl, then add the thin part of the milk with the chicken stock. Add the Chinese leaves, sugar and salt and bring to the boil. Simmer for 6–8 minutes.

4 Turn out on to a serving dish, halve the quails' eggs and toss in the sauce. Scatter with the spring onions and the shredded coconut and serve.

Octopus and Red Wine Stew

Unless you are happy to clean and prepare octopus for this Greek dish, buy one that is ready for cooking.

INGREDIENTS

Serves 4

900g/2lb prepared octopus
450g/1lb onions, sliced
2 bay leaves
450g/1lb ripe tomatoes
60ml/4 tbsp olive oil
4 garlic cloves, crushed
5ml/1 tsp caster sugar
15ml/1 tbsp chopped fresh oregano
   or rosemary
30ml/2 tbsp chopped fresh parsley
150ml/¼ pint/⅔ cup red wine
30ml/2 tbsp red wine vinegar
chopped fresh herbs, to garnish
warm bread and pine nuts, to serve

1 Put the octopus in a saucepan of gently simmering water with one-quarter of the sliced onions and the bay leaves. Cook gently for 1 hour.

2 While the octopus is cooking, plunge the tomatoes into boiling water for 30 seconds, then refresh in cold water. Peel away the skins and chop roughly.

3 Drain the octopus and, using a sharp knife, cut it into bite-sized pieces. Discard the onions and bay leaves.

4 Heat the oil in a saucepan and fry the octopus, the remaining chopped onions and the crushed garlic for 3 minutes. Add the tomatoes, sugar, oregano or rosemary, parsley, wine and vinegar and cook, stirring constantly, for 5 minutes until the mixture is pulpy.

5 Cover the pan and cook over the lowest possible heat for about 1½ hours, until the sauce is thickened and the octopus is tender. Garnish with fresh herbs and serve with plenty of warm bread and pine nuts to scatter over the top.

Louisiana Seafood Gumbo

Gumbo has the consistency of soup, but is served over rice as a main course. This recipe is based on one created by chef John Folse, of the renowned Louisiana restaurant Lafitte's Landing. In his neck of the bayous, where they are cheap and plentiful, oysters are an important ingredient. However, his suggestion to substitute mussels for oysters works very well too.

INGREDIENTS

Serves 6

450g/1lb mussels

250ml/8fl oz/1 cup water

450g/1lb prawns

1 cooked crab weighing about
   1kg/2¼lb

1 small bunch parsley, leaves
   chopped and stems reserved

150ml/¼ pint/⅔ cup cooking oil

115g/4oz/1 cup plain flour

1 green pepper, seeded and chopped

1 large onion, chopped

2 celery sticks, sliced

3 garlic cloves, finely chopped

75g/3oz smoked spiced sausage, skinned
   and sliced

6 spring onions, chopped

cayenne pepper

Tabasco sauce

salt

boiled rice, to serve

1 Scrub the mussels in cold water and debeard. Discard any that are broken or any that do not close immediately when sharply tapped.

2 Heat the water in a deep saucepan. When it boils, add the mussels, cover tightly and cook over a high heat, shaking regularly, for 3 minutes. As the mussels open, lift them out with tongs into a strainer set over a bowl. Discard any that do not open after a further 1 minute's cooking.

3 Shell the mussels. Return the liquid from the bowl to the pan and make up to 2 litres/3½ pints/ 9 cups with water. Shell the prawns and put the shells and heads into the pan. Remove and separate the brown and white meat from the crab. Add the pieces of shell to the saucepan with 10ml/2 tsp salt.

4 Bring the shellfish stock to the boil, skimming off any froth that rises to the surface. When no more froth rises, add the parsley stalks and simmer for 15 minutes. Cool, then drain off the liquid, discarding the solids. Make the shellfish stock up to 2 litres/ 3½ pints/9 cups with water.

5 Heat the oil in a heavy-based saucepan and stir in the flour. Cook, stirring constantly, until golden-brown in colour. It is essential to stir constantly to darken the roux without burning. Should black specks occur at any stage of cooking, you must discard the roux and start again.

6 As soon as the roux is the right colour, add the pepper, onion, celery and garlic and cook for about 3 minutes, until they are soft. (It is important that they are added the moment the roux is the right colour, as this arrests its darkening.) Then add the sausage. Reheat the stock.

7 Stir the brown crabmeat into the roux, then ladle in the hot stock, a little at a time, stirring constantly until it is all smoothly incorporated. Bring to the boil and simmer gently for 30 minutes, partially covered.

8 Add the prawns, mussels, white crabmeat and spring onions. Return to the boil, season with salt if necessary, cayenne and a dash or two of Tabasco sauce and simmer for a further minute.

9 Add the chopped parsley leaves and serve immediately, ladling the gumbo over the hot rice in soup plates.

PASTA,
NOODLE &
RICE DISHES

~

Spaghetti with Hot-and-sour Fish

A truly Chinese spicy taste is what makes this sauce so different.

Serves 4

350g/12oz spaghetti tricolore

450g/1lb monkfish, skinned

225g/8oz courgettes

1 fresh green chilli, cored and seeded

15ml/1 tbsp olive oil

1 large onion, chopped

5ml/1 tsp turmeric

115g/4oz shelled peas, thawed if frozen

10ml/2 tsp lemon juice

75ml/5 tbsp hoisin sauce

150ml/¼ pint/⅔ cup water

salt and freshly ground black pepper

dill sprig, to garnish

1 Cook the pasta in boiling salted water according to the instructions on the packet, until tender, but still firm to the bite.

2 Meanwhile, with a sharp knife, cut the monkfish into bite-sized pieces.

COOK'S TIP

∼

This dish is quite low in calories, so it is ideal for slimmers. Hoisin sauce is widely available from most supermarkets or Chinese food stores.

3 Thinly slice the courgettes, then finely chop the fresh, green chilli.

4 Heat the oil in a large frying pan and fry the onion for 5 minutes until softened, but not coloured. Add the turmeric.

5 Add the chilli, courgettes and peas and fry over a medium heat for about 5 minutes until the vegetables have softened.

6 Stir in the fish, lemon juice, hoisin sauce and water. Bring to the boil, then simmer for about 5 minutes, or until the fish is tender. Season to taste.

7 Drain the pasta thoroughly and turn it into a serving bowl. Toss in the sauce to coat. Serve at once, garnished with fresh dill.

Tagliatelle with Smoked Salmon

This is a pretty pasta sauce that tastes as good as it looks. The light texture of the cucumber perfectly complements the fish. Different effects and colour combinations can be achieved by using green, white or red tagliatelle – or even a mixture of all three.

INGREDIENTS

Serves 4

350g/12oz dried or fresh tagliatelle
½ cucumber
75g/3oz butter
grated rind of 1 orange
30ml/2 tbsp chopped fresh dill
300ml/½ pint/1¼ cups single cream
15ml/1 tbsp orange juice
115g/4oz smoked salmon, skinned
salt and freshly ground black pepper

1 If using dried pasta, cook in lightly salted boiling water following the manufacturer's instructions on the packet. If using fresh pasta, cook in lightly salted boiling water for 2–3 minutes, or until just tender but still firm to the bite.

2 Using a sharp knife, cut the cucumber in half lengthways, then using a small spoon scoop out the cucumber seeds and discard.

3 Turn the cucumber on to the flat side and slice it thinly.

4 Melt the butter in a heavy-based saucepan, add the grated orange rind and fresh dill and stir well. Add the cucumber and cook gently over a low heat for about 2 minutes, stirring from time to time.

5 Add the cream, orange juice and seasoning to taste and simmer gently for 1 minute.

6 Meanwhile, cut the salmon into thin strips.

7 Stir the salmon into the sauce and heat through.

8 Drain the pasta thoroughly and toss it in the sauce. Serve immediately.

COOK'S TIP

A more economical way to make this special-occasion sauce is to use smoked salmon pieces, sold relatively inexpensively by most delicatessens and some super-markets. (These are just off-cuts and awkwardly shaped pieces that are unsuitable for recipes requiring whole slices of smoked salmon.) Smoked trout is a less expensive alternative, but it lacks the rich flavour and colour of smoked salmon.

Black Pasta with Squid Sauce

Tagliatelle flavoured with squid ink looks amazing and tastes deliciously of the sea. You'll find it in good Italian delicatessens.

INGREDIENTS

Serves 4

105ml/7 tbsp olive oil

2 shallots, chopped

2 garlic cloves, crushed

45ml/3 tbsp chopped fresh parsley

675g/1½lb cleaned squid, cut into rings and rinsed

150ml/¼ pint/⅔ cup dry white wine

400g/14oz can chopped tomatoes

2.5ml/½ tsp dried chilli flakes or powder

450g/1lb black tagliatelle

salt and fresh ground black pepper

1 Heat the oil in a pan and add the shallots. Cook until pale golden in colour, then add the garlic. When the garlic colours a little, add 30ml/2 tbsp of the parsley, stir, then add the squid and stir again. Cook for 3–4 minutes, then add the wine.

2 Simmer for a few seconds, then add the tomatoes and chilli flakes or powder and season with salt and pepper to taste. Cover and simmer gently for about 1 hour, until the squid is tender. Add more water if necessary.

3 Cook the pasta in plenty of boiling salted water, according to the instructions on the packet, until tender, but still firm to the bite. Drain and return the pasta to the pan. Add the squid sauce and mix well. Sprinkle each serving with the remaining chopped parsley and serve at once.

COOK'S TIP

The labelling of olive oil can be confusing. The oil is basically divided into two types – pure and virgin. The latter comes from the first pressing, but virgin olive oil is further sub-divided, according to its level of acidity. The least acid and so the best oil is extra virgin. Use this quality for special dishes and salad dressings, but the next best oil – virgin – may be used for general cooking. Pure olive oil, although not in any way adulterated, lacks the unique flavour of virgin oil.

Pasta with Scallops in Tomato Sauce

Delicate and simple, this pasta dish makes a good starter or main dish.

INGREDIENTS

Serves 4

450g/1lb long, thin pasta, such as fettucine
   or linguine
30ml/2 tbsp olive oil
2 garlic cloves, finely chopped
450g/1lb prepared scallops, sliced in
   half horizontally
30ml/2 tbsp chopped fresh basil
salt and freshly ground black pepper
salt
fresh basil sprigs, to garnish

For the sauce

30ml/2 tbsp olive oil
½ onion, finely chopped
1 garlic clove, finely chopped
2 x 400g/14oz cans peeled tomatoes

1 To make the sauce, heat the oil in a non-stick frying pan. Add the onion, garlic and a little salt, and cook for about 5 minutes, stirring occasionally, until just softened, but not coloured.

2 Add the tomatoes, with their juice, and crush with a fork. Bring to the boil, then lower the heat and simmer gently for 15 minutes. Remove the pan from the heat and set aside.

3 Bring a large pan of salted water to the boil. Add the pasta and cook until just tender to the bite, according to the instructions on the packet.

4 Meanwhile, combine the oil and garlic in another non-stick frying pan and cook for about 30 seconds, until just sizzling. Add the scallops and 2.5ml/½ tsp salt and cook over a high heat for about 3 minutes, tossing, until the scallops are cooked through.

5 Add the scallops to the tomato sauce. Season with salt and pepper to taste, then stir gently and keep warm.

6 Drain the pasta, rinse under hot water, and drain. Add the scallop sauce and the basil and toss thoroughly. Serve immediately, garnished with fresh basil sprigs.

Baked Seafood Spaghetti

In this dish, each portion is baked and served in an individual parcel, which is then opened at the table. Use oven parchment or aluminium foil to make the parcels.

INGREDIENTS

Serves 4

450g/1lb fresh mussels
120ml/4fl oz/½ cup dry white wine
60ml/4 tbsp olive oil
2 garlic cloves, finely chopped
450g/1lb tomatoes, fresh or canned, peeled and finely chopped
400g/14oz spaghetti or other long pasta
225g/8oz fresh or frozen and thawed, uncooked peeled prawns, deveined
30ml/2 tbsp chopped fresh parsley
salt and freshly ground black pepper

1 Scrub the mussels well under cold running water, cutting off the beards with a small sharp knife. Discard any with broken shells or which do not close immediately when sharply tapped. Place the mussels and the wine in a large saucepan and heat until they open.

2 Lift out the mussels and remove to a side dish. Discard any that do not open. Strain the cooking liquid through clean muslin to remove any grit and reserve until needed.

3 In a medium saucepan, heat the oil and garlic together for 1–2 minutes. Add the tomatoes, and cook over moderate to high heat until they soften. Stir in 175ml/6fl oz/¾ cup of the reserved cooking liquid from the mussels and simmer gently.

4 Meanwhile, cook the pasta in a large pan of boiling salted water, according to the packet instructions, until tender, but still firm to the bite.

5 Just before draining the pasta, add the prawns and parsley to the tomato sauce. Simmer for a further 2 minutes, or until the prawns are cooked through. Taste and adjust the seasoning, if necessary. Remove from the heat and set aside. Drain the pasta.

6 Prepare 4 pieces of parchment paper or foil approximately 30cm x 45cm (12in x 18in). Place each sheet in the centre of a shallow bowl. Turn the drained pasta into a mixing bowl. Add the tomato sauce and mix well. Stir in the mussels.

7 Divide the pasta and seafood between the 4 pieces of paper or foil, placing a mound in the centre of each, and twisting the paper ends together to make a closed packet. (The bowl under the paper will stop the sauce from spilling while the paper parcels are being closed.) Arrange on a large baking tray and bake in a preheated oven at 150°C/300°F/ Gas 2 for 8–10 minutes. Place an unopened packet on each of 4 individual serving plates.

Seafood Laska

For a special occasion serve creamy rice noodles in a spicy, coconut-flavoured broth, topped with a selection of seafood. There is a fair amount of work involved in the preparation, but you can make the soup base ahead.

INGREDIENTS

Serves 4

4 fresh red chillies, seeded and
   roughly chopped
1 onion, roughly chopped
1 piece blacan, the size of a stock cube
1 lemon grass stalk, chopped
1 small piece fresh root ginger,
   roughly chopped
6 macadamia nuts or almonds
60ml/4 tbsp vegetable oil
5ml/1 tsp paprika
5ml/1 tsp ground turmeric
475ml/16fl oz/2 cups stock or water
600ml/1 pint/2½ cups coconut milk
fish sauce (see method)
12 raw king prawns, peeled and deveined
8 scallops
225g/8oz prepared squid, cut into rings
350g/12oz rice vermicelli or rice noodles,
   soaked in warm water until soft
salt and freshly ground black pepper
lime halves, to serve

For the garnish
¼ cucumber, cut into matchsticks
2 fresh red chillies, seeded and
   finely sliced
30ml/2 tbsp mint leaves
30ml/2 tbsp fried shallots

COOK'S TIP

Blacan is dried shrimp or prawn paste. It is sold in small blocks and you will find it in oriental supermarkets.

---

1 In a blender or food processor, process the chillies, onion, blacan, lemon grass, ginger and nuts until smooth in texture.

2 Heat 45ml/3 tbsp of the oil in a large saucepan. Add the chilli paste and fry for 6 minutes. Stir in the paprika and turmeric and fry for about 2 minutes more.

3 Add the stock or water and the coconut milk to the pan. Bring to the boil, reduce the heat and simmer gently for 15–20 minutes. Season to taste with the fish sauce.

4 Season the seafood with salt and pepper. Heat the remaining oil in a frying pan, add the seafood and stir-fry quickly for 2–3 minutes until cooked.

5 Add the noodles to the broth and heat through. Divide among individual serving bowls. Place the fried seafood on top, then garnish with the cucumber, chillies, mint and fried shallots. Serve with the limes.

Bamie Goreng

This fried noodle dish from Indonesia is wonderfully accommodating. To the basic recipe you can add other vegetables, such as mushrooms, broccoli, leeks or beansprouts, if you prefer. You can use whatever you have to hand, bearing in mind the importance of achieving a balance of colours, flavours and textures.

INGREDIENTS

Serves 6–8

450g/1lb dried egg noodles
1 boneless, skinless chicken breast
115g/4oz pork fillet
115g/4oz calves' liver (optional)
2 eggs, beaten
90ml/6 tbsp oil
25g/1oz butter or margarine
2 garlic cloves, crushed
115g/4oz cooked peeled prawns
115g/4oz spinach or Chinese leaves
2 celery sticks, finely sliced
4 spring onions, shredded
about 60ml/4 tbsp chicken stock
dark soy sauce and light soy sauce
salt and freshly ground black pepper
deep-fried onions and celery leaves,
    to garnish
mixed fruit and vegetable salad, to
    serve (optional)

1 Cook the noodles in lightly salted, boiling water for 3–4 minutes. Drain, rinse with cold water and drain well again. Set aside until required.

2 Finely slice the chicken, pork fillet and calves' liver, if using.

3 Season the eggs. Heat 5ml/1 tsp of the oil with the butter or margarine in a small pan until melted. Stir in the eggs and keep stirring until scrambled. Set aside.

4 Heat the remaining oil in a preheated wok and stir-fry the garlic with the chicken, pork and liver for 2–3 minutes, until they have changed colour. Stir in the prawns, spinach or Chinese leaves, celery and spring onions.

5 Add the drained noodles and toss the mixture well so that all the ingredients are thoroughly combined. Add just enough stock to moisten and add dark and light soy sauce to taste. Finally, stir in the scrambled eggs.

6 Garnish the dish with deep-fried onions and celery leaves. Serve with a mixed fruit and vegetable salad, if liked.

Seafood Chow Mein

This basic recipe can be adapted using a range of different items for the 'dressing'.

INGREDIENTS

Serves 4

75g/3oz squid, cleaned

75g/3oz raw prawns

3–4 fresh scallops, prepared

½ egg white

15ml/1 tbsp cornflour paste

250g/9oz egg noodles

75–90ml/5–6 tbsp vegetable oil

50g/2oz mangetouts

2.5ml/½ tsp salt

2.5ml/½ tsp light brown sugar

15ml/1 tbsp Chinese rice wine or
    dry sherry

30ml/2 tbsp light soy sauce

2 spring onions, finely shredded

vegetable or chicken stock, if necessary

few drops sesame oil

1 Open up the squid and, using a sharp knife, score the inside in a criss-cross pattern. Cut the squid into pieces, each about the size of a postage stamp. Soak the squid in a bowl of boiling water until all the pieces curl up. Rinse in cold water and drain.

2 Peel and devein the prawns, then cut each of them in half lengthways.

3 Cut each scallop into 3–4 slices. Mix the scallops and prawns with the egg white and cornflour paste and set aside.

4 Cook the noodles in boiling water according to the packet instructions, then drain and rinse under cold water. Mix with about 15ml/1 tbsp of the oil.

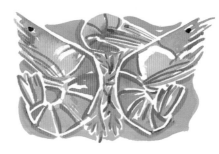

COOK'S TIP

To make cornflour paste, mix 4 parts dry cornflour with about 5 parts cold water until smooth.

5 Heat about 30–45ml/2–3 tbsp of the oil in a preheated wok until hot. Stir-fry the mangetouts and seafood for about 2 minutes, then add the salt, sugar, rice wine or sherry, half of the soy sauce and about half of the spring onions. Blend well and add a little stock, if necessary. Remove and keep warm.

6 Heat the remaining oil in the wok and stir-fry the noodles for 2–3 minutes with the remaining soy sauce. Place in a large serving dish, pour the 'dressing' on top, garnish with the remaining spring onions and sprinkle with sesame oil. Serve hot or cold.

Buckwheat Noodles with Smoked Trout

The light, crisp texture of the pak choi balances the strong, earthy flavours of the mushrooms, the buckwheat noodles and the smokiness of the trout.

INGREDIENTS

Serves 4

350g/12oz buckwheat noodles
30ml/2 tbsp vegetable oil
115g/4oz fresh shiitake mushrooms, quartered
2 garlic cloves, finely chopped
15ml/1 tbsp grated fresh root ginger
225g/8oz pak choi
1 spring onion, finely sliced diagonally
15ml/1 tbsp dark sesame oil
30ml/2 tbsp mirin
30ml/2 tbsp soy sauce
2 smoked trout, skinned and boned
salt and freshly ground black pepper
30ml/2 tbsp coriander leaves and 10ml/ 2 tsp sesame seeds, toasted, to garnish

1 Cook the buckwheat noodles in a saucepan of boiling water for about 7–10 minutes, or until just tender, according to the packet instructions.

2 Meanwhile, heat the oil in a large frying pan. Add the shiitake mushrooms and sauté over a medium heat for 3 minutes. Add the garlic, ginger and pak choi, and continue to sauté for a further 2 minutes.

3 Drain the noodles and add them to the mushroom mixture, with the spring onion, sesame oil, mirin and soy sauce. Toss and season with salt and pepper to taste.

4 Break up the trout into bite-sized pieces. Arrange the noodle mixture on individual serving plates and top with trout.

5 Garnish the noodles with coriander leaves and sesame seeds and serve immediately.

COOK'S TIP
~
Mirin is sweet, cooking sake, available from Japanese stores.

Stir-fried Noodles with Sweet Salmon

A delicious sauce forms the marinade for the salmon in this recipe. Served with soft-fried noodles, it makes a stunning dish.

INGREDIENTS

Serves 4

350g/12oz salmon fillet

30ml/2 tbsp Japanese soy sauce (shoyu)

30ml/2 tbsp sake

60ml/4 tbsp mirin or sweet sherry

5ml/1 tsp light brown soft sugar

10ml/2 tsp grated fresh root ginger

3 cloves garlic, 1 crushed, and 2 sliced into rounds

30ml/2 tbsp groundnut oil

225g/8oz dried egg noodles, cooked and drained

50g/2oz alfalfa sprouts

30ml/2 tbsp sesame seeds, lightly toasted

1 Thinly slice the salmon, then place in a shallow dish.

2 In a bowl, mix together the soy sauce, sake, mirin or sherry, sugar, ginger and crushed garlic. Pour over the salmon, cover and leave to marinate for 30 minutes.

3 Drain the salmon, scraping off and reserving the marinade. Place the salmon in a single layer on a baking sheet. Cook under a preheated grill for 2–3 minutes, without turning.

4 Meanwhile, heat a wok until hot, add the oil and swirl it around. Add the garlic rounds and cook until golden brown, but do not allow them to burn.

5 Add the cooked noodles and reserved marinade to the wok. Stir-fry for 3–4 minutes, until the marinade has reduced slightly to make a syrupy glaze that coats the egg noodles.

6 Toss in the alfalfa sprouts, then remove immediately from the heat. Transfer to warmed serving plates and top with the salmon. Sprinkle over the toasted sesame seeds. Serve at once.

COOK'S TIP
∾

It is important to scrape the marinade off the fish as any remaining pieces of ginger or garlic would burn during grilling and spoil the finished dish.

Salmon Risotto

Any rice can be used for risotto, although the creamiest ones are made with short grain arborio and carnaroli rice. Fresh tarragon and cucumber combine well to bring out the flavour of the salmon.

INGREDIENTS

Serves 4

25g/1oz butter

1 small bunch spring onions, white part only, chopped

½ cucumber, peeled, seeded and chopped

400g/14oz short grain arborio or carnaroli rice

900ml/1½ pints/3¾ cups chicken or fish stock

150ml/¼ pint/⅔ cup dry white wine

450g/1lb salmon fillet, skinned and diced

45ml/3 tbsp chopped fresh tarragon

1 Heat the butter in a large saucepan and add the spring onions and cucumber. Cook for 2–3 minutes without colouring.

2 Add the rice, chicken or fish stock and wine, bring to the boil and simmer, uncovered, for 10 minutes, stirring occasionally.

3 Stir in the diced salmon and chopped tarragon. Continue cooking for a further 5 minutes, then switch off the heat. Cover the pan and leave to stand for 5 minutes before serving.

VARIATION

Long grain rice can also be used. Choose grains that have not been pre-cooked and reduce the stock to 750ml/1¼ pints/3 cups per 400g/14oz of rice.

Fish with Rice

This Arabic fish dish, Sayadieh, is very popular in the Lebanon.

INGREDIENTS

Serves 4–6

juice of 1 lemon

45ml/3 tbsp oil

900g/2lb cod steaks

4 large onions, chopped

5ml/1 tsp ground cumin

2–3 saffron strands, soaked in 30ml/2 tbsp hot water

1 litre/1¾ pints/4 cups fish stock

500g/1¼lb basmati or other long grain rice

115g/4oz pine nuts, lightly toasted

salt and freshly ground black pepper

fresh parsley, to garnish

1 Blend together the lemon juice and 15ml/1 tbsp of the oil in a shallow dish. Add the fish steaks, turning to coat, then cover and set aside to marinate for 30 minutes.

2 Heat the remaining oil in a large saucepan or flameproof casserole and fry the onions for 5–6 minutes until softened and golden, stirring occasionally.

3 Drain the fish, reserving the marinade, and add to the pan. Fry for 1–2 minutes on each side until lightly golden, then add the cumin, saffron strands and a little salt and pepper.

4 Pour in the fish stock and the reserved marinade, bring to the boil and then simmer very gently, over a low heat, for 5–10 minutes, until the fish is nearly done.

5 Transfer the fish to a plate and add the rice to the stock. Bring to the boil, then reduce the heat and simmer very gently over a low heat for 15 minutes until nearly all the stock has been absorbed.

6 Arrange the fish on the rice and cover. Steam over a low heat for another 15–20 minutes.

7 Transfer the fish to a plate, then spoon the rice on to a large flat dish and arrange the fish on top. Sprinkle with lightly toasted pine nuts and garnish with fresh parsley.

COOK'S TIP
Take care when cooking the rice that the saucepan does not boil dry. Check it occasionally and add more stock or water, if it becomes necessary.

Mixed Fish Jambalaya

Jambalaya, from New Orleans, is not unlike a paella, but much spicier. The name comes from the French word 'jambon', and tells us that the dish was originally based on ham, but you can add many other ingredients of your choice, including fish and shellfish.

INGREDIENTS

Serves 4

30ml/2 tbsp oil

115g/4oz smoked bacon, rinded and diced

1 onion, chopped

2 sticks celery, chopped

2 large garlic cloves, chopped

5ml/1 tsp cayenne pepper

2 bay leaves

5ml/1 tsp dried oregano

2.5ml/½ tsp dried thyme

4 tomatoes, skinned and chopped

150ml/¼ pint/⅔ cup ready-made
   tomato sauce

350g/12oz long grain rice

475ml/16fl oz/2 cups fish stock

175g/6oz firm white fish (coley, cod, saithe
   or haddock), skinned, boned and cubed

115g/4oz cooked peeled prawns

salt and freshly ground black pepper

2 chopped spring onions, to garnish

1 Heat the oil in a large saucepan and fry the bacon until crisp. Add the onion and celery and stir until they begin to stick to the base of the pan.

2 Add the garlic, cayenne pepper, herbs, tomatoes and seasoning and mix well. Stir in the tomato sauce, rice and stock and bring to the boil.

3 Gently stir in the fish and transfer to an ovenproof dish. Cover tightly with foil and bake in a preheated oven at 180°C/350°F/ Gas 4 for 20–30 minutes, until the rice is just tender. Stir in the prawns and heat through. Serve sprinkled with the spring onions.

Spanish Seafood Paella

Paella is also the name of the heavy, cast-iron pan in which this dish is traditionally cooked.

Serves 4

60ml/4 tbsp olive oil

225g/8oz monkfish or cod, skinned and cut into chunks

3 prepared baby squid, body cut into rings and tentacles chopped

1 red mullet, filleted, skinned and cut into chunks (optional)

1 onion, chopped

3 garlic cloves, finely chopped

1 red pepper, seeded and sliced

4 tomatoes, skinned and chopped

225g/8oz arborio rice

450ml/¾ pint/1⅞ cups fish stock

150ml/¼ pint/⅔ cup white wine

75g/3oz frozen peas

4–5 saffron strands soaked in 30ml/2 tbsp hot water

115g/4oz cooked peeled prawns

8 fresh mussels in shells, scrubbed

salt and freshly ground black pepper

15ml/1 tbsp chopped fresh parsley, to garnish

lemon wedges, to serve

1 Heat 30ml/2 tbsp of the olive oil in a large frying pan and add the monkfish or cod, the squid and the red mullet, if using. Stir-fry for 2 minutes, then transfer the fish to a bowl with all the juices and set aside.

2 Heat the remaining 30ml/2 tbsp of oil in the pan and add the onion, garlic and red pepper. Fry for 6–7 minutes, stirring frequently, until the onion and pepper have softened.

3 Stir in the tomatoes and fry for 2 minutes, then add the rice, stirring to coat the grains with oil, and cook for 2–3 minutes. Pour on the fish stock and wine and add the peas, saffron and water. Season well and mix.

4 Gently stir in the fish with all the juices, followed by the prawns and then push the mussels into the rice. Cover and cook over a gentle heat for about 30 minutes, or until the stock has been absorbed but the mixture is still moist.

5 Remove from the heat, keep covered and leave to stand for 5 minutes. Discard any mussels that do not open. Sprinkle the paella with parsley and serve with lemon wedges.

Index